CANCELLED

Up in Smoke

CANCELLED

Up in Smoke

Stories from a life on fire

Leigh Hosy-Pickett

First published in Great Britain in 2022 by Trapeze,
an imprint of The Orion Publishing Group Ltd
Carmelite House, 50 Victoria Embankment
London EC4Y 0DZ

An Hachette UK Company

1 3 5 7 9 10 8 6 4 2

Copyright © Leigh Hosy-Pickett 2022

The moral right of Leigh Hosy-Pickett to be identified as
the author of this work has been asserted in accordance
with the Copyright, Designs and Patents Act of 1988.

All rights reserved. No part of this publication may be
reproduced, stored in a retrieval system, or transmitted
in any form or by any means, electronic, mechanical,
photocopying, recording, or otherwise, without the
prior permission of both the copyright owner and the
above publisher of this book.

A CIP catalogue record for this book is
available from the British Library.

ISBN (Hardback) 978 1 4091 9885 7
ISBN (Export Trade Paperback) 978 1 4091 9886 4
ISBN (eBook) 978 1 4091 9888 8
ISBN (Audio) 978 1 4091 9889 5

Typeset by Born Group
Printed and bound in Great Britain by Clays Ltd, Elcograf S.p.A.

MIX
Paper from
responsible sources
FSC® C104740
FSC www.fsc.org

Falkirk Council	
30124 03169569 7	
Askews & Holts	
B HOS	£18.99
MK	

This book is dedicated to firefighters everywhere. And to every single control-room operator, police officer, medic, coastguard, lifeboat crew and mountain rescue team. You are everyday heroes and make me proud to be associated through our 999 number.

To respect the privacy of all those I have encountered in my twenty five years as a firefighter, I have altered various details of people, places and incidents. Despite these changes, this book is an entirely authentic representation of the highs and lows of life as a firefighter. From tears of sadness, to tears of laughter, I celebrate the extraordinary selflessness and bravery of my firefighting brothers and sisters, particularly those I have been lucky enough to call friends and colleagues.

Contents

I

This Is Not a Drill

Sometimes you just know when a situation is going to go bad. There can be all sorts of different things that trigger it – the colour of smoke coming from under a closed door, the feeling of a building shifting as you run up the stairwell, or the smell of petrol as you crawl into the wreckage of a car. That familiar feeling in the pit of your stomach, that primal survival instinct honed by years of professional experience, that little voice: *Hurry up, you haven't got long.*

This time, what triggered it was the DJ putting on 'Do Ya Think I'm Sexy?' by Rod Stewart.

To be fair, there'd already been early warning signs.

My watch had to carry out a 'During Performance' inspection – a safety check, where it was our role to observe a business as it operated at maximum capacity.[1] Given the nature of these visits, our arrival was planned

---

1 For those readers blissfully unaware of the staffing rhythms of the Fire Brigade, a watch is a team of firefighters. There are usually four watches aligned with each station – red, white, green and blue. Each watch rotates across an identical shift pattern of two working days, followed by two working nights. They will then have four – extremely necessary – days off.

to coincide with the place at its busiest. This was the best way to judge how safe their setup was, as well as check the place wasn't overly packed. Basically, the whole point was not to give them too much warning that you were coming, giving them time to prepare – unlock fire doors, tidy away beer crates from fire escape corridors, that sort of thing.

For that reason, my watch hadn't rocked up to the local nightclub in a pump (fire engine) with its blue lights flashing, all of us dressed in our personal protective equipment, helmets and breathing apparatus.[2] Instead, we'd arrived in blue shirts, black ties, epaulets, shiny shoes and peaked officer caps, though the most giveaway detail was our clipboards and pens. It was my first time out on Fire Service inspection duty and I was feeling pretty important. As we pushed our way onto the dance floor to find a person of authority, I noticed one or two clubgoers staring and pointing.

This could get interesting, I thought, but back then I was young, right at the very beginning of my career, a recruit not yet experienced enough to properly spot the signs of approaching danger. On this particular occasion, the venue we were attending was a bit of a zoo, the kind of establishment you might have seen on *Geordie Shore* and then, a few pints later, *Crimewatch*. By happy accident our 11 p.m. arrival seemed to have coincided with more than half the club deciding it was time for shots. The atmosphere was equal parts Jägermeister and

---

2 A 'pump' is our word for a fire engine, but it can also be referred to as an 'appliance'.

hairspray – to be honest, I could have done with my breathing apparatus.

I watched as people were beginning to nudge each other and started to pay a bit more attention to our surroundings. Just about everybody in the club was female and I was able to count at least two wedding veils and learner plate combos across the bar. It was at that point that I started to get the first tingles of warning. I spotted the DJ, who had also spotted us, and at that exact moment he seemed to be adding two to two to make twenty-two.

Oh no, I thought, the precariousness of our situation finally hitting home. *Don't you say it.*

But it was too late. Madonna's 'Vogue' scratched to an end and the metallic squeak of a microphone being switched on cut through the speakers. *Bang!* A spotlight had been trained on me, pinning me to the spot. I felt emotionally exposed. That sensation was about to get physical.

'Girls, we've got a special surprise for you,' yelled a voice through the speakers. 'Your strippers are here!' Then the opening bars of Rod Stewart.

What a knobhead!

Even if you haven't been involved personally, every firefighter has heard tell of the legend of the time a drunken room has mistaken a team of firefighters for strippers. There are stories of crews at work having their clothes torn off, their torsos scratched to pieces. The fact that this takes place to a soundtrack of Shaggy's 'It Wasn't Me', or 'I Will Survive' by Gloria Gaynor only adds to the humiliation. But it's one thing to hear about it and a very different one to live it. The crowd immediately swarmed in. In the crush, one of the lads grabbed me by the arm.

'Leigh, quick, let's go find someone in charge . . .'

I nodded, as we made our way slowly out through the crowd, partly checking for out-of-date fire extinguishers and blocked exit routes, partly just trying to escape the long-nailed hands that kept on reaching out towards us . . . and straight into one of the hen dos.

Several years ago, when times were a little less politically correct, the deodorant brand, Lynx, ran a particularly effective advertising campaign. In a series of TV clips, a man – sometimes on a beach, other times filmed in a park – was shown spraying a gallon of the whiffy stuff under his armpits and across his Ryan Giggs-style chest rug. Suddenly, from off-camera, the sound of galloping feet rumbled into earshot as an army of scantily clad women, drawn to the intoxicating pong of mass-market deodorant, threw themselves at the wearer. The phenomenon was named 'The Lynx Effect'.

The deodorant was, in my personal opinion, horrible stuff – its pungent odour swept through pubs and dance floors across the country. But The Lynx Effect was just about the most effective marketing idea imaginable. Blokes everywhere bought up the stuff by the shopping basket load, many of them expecting to be mobbed by packs of adoring models. Suddenly, in this nightclub, I'd been presented with the literal embodiment of what had once been an ad director's flash of inspiration. And it was nothing like it was on TV. The crowd turned towards me as one, arms outstretched like a horde of drunken zombies.

Someone screamed sultrily in my ear, 'Are you really a stripper?'

'Too right he is!' shouted another voice behind me as a hand grabbed at my cap and sent it spinning across the club like a frisby. 'Get yer kit off then!'

Surrounded, I looked around for backup, mumbling that I was, in fact, a firefighter, hoping for a more experienced colleague with the wisdom and moral fortitude to rescue me. But I saw we had all been taken down, one by one: my watch was pulled under, clothes torn from their backs in an undignified assault. My tie was ripped away and turned into a headscarf. A pair of hands grabbed my shirt and yanked, hard, popping the buttons away. My trousers followed the same path. I was about to surrender my dignity entirely when the house lights came up. *We were saved!* The club owner, having caught sight of the shit show, and a potential lawsuit, was calling time on the party in a panic.

'Ladies, these are not strippers!' he shouted. 'It's the actual Fire Brigade. They've come to do an inspection of our club.'

A wave of shock rippled round the dance floor as the crazed throng took one, two, three steps back in horror. I heard one or two mumbled apologies. As the crowd receded, it became clear that my colleagues had all been better than me at keeping hold of their clothes. My hat, all bent out of shape, was plopped back on my head, my tie draped over my shoulder. As I started to shuffle back into my returned clothes, someone pinched me on the arse, muttering 'Shame!' I puffed out a sigh of relief. I was battle-scarred for sure, but unbroken and still composed enough to return to the business of checking for out-of-date fire extinguishers and padlocked fire exits, thankful that 'During Performance' inspections came but once a year.

The club passed with flying colours but the sound of Rod Stewart's raspy tones still brings me out in a cold sweat.

My name's Leigh and I have the best job in the world. Fire, or the control of it, has been my occupation for over twenty-five years. I've spent most of my adult life responding to the kind of damage that a carelessly discarded cigarette causes. I've cut people free from the tangled messes of what used to be cars. I've watched smoke clear in more sorts of rooms than I care to remember. I've lived a life where intense periods of waiting around have been interspersed with life at its most extreme. I've known that every meal with my wife and kids might be my last. I've witnessed the most extreme acts of bravery and listened to colleagues, men and women who've seen things no person should ever see. I've watched people get back up and keep going when they're out on their feet, feeling unable to continue, because that's the job.

For most people, a mistake at work is an email accidentally sent to the whole company, but for us it can be the difference between life and death. The difference between finding that hunched shape in the smoke. That feeling of relief. Carrying them out to the ambulance, to the oxygen mask, the squeeze of your hand, them mouthing 'thank you'. Back to the station, the jokes, the voices loud from adrenaline, the shower water swirling around your feet, dirty with smoke. The good nights. Stopping as you put the kids to bed, or order a takeaway and remembering what you did that day. The nights sat up at the kitchen table, staring into space, replaying again and again what you could have done differently . . .

But it's what I do. The family business, if you like. I'm a third-generation firefighter, my dad and grandad both firefighters before me, all of us operating from the same fire station since 1968. I followed in their sooty footsteps, working my way up from a recruit and probationary firefighter to my current position as a Watch Commander. What inspired me? I grew up witnessing firefighters as caring and heroic figures, respected in their communities, fulfilling a role that the majority of people would rarely consider.[3]

Being a firefighter is an interesting job. There are no nicknames like 'The Plod' or 'The Rozzers' but we're not the same level of national treasure as a doctor or nurse either. For most people, most of the time, coming into contact with a firefighter is a rare occurrence and not one they think about very often.[4] But the odds are, if you meet me in my fire-gear you're probably having some version of a bad day.[5] For some people, that might

---

3 And yes, I've heard every hose joke imaginable.

4 And if you want to keep it that way – buy a smoke alarm and check the batteries by testing it weekly. We're going to keep coming back to this throughout the book.

5 Unless you think I'm a stripper.

be the inconvenience of some smoke damage in the kitchen, for others it will be the moment their entire life changes forever.

With this book I want to tell stories that show the full spectrum of what it is to be a firefighter. People really only concentrate on the pure adrenaline of it – the burning buildings and the decisions under pressure. But that's only part of being a firefighter, I want to tell the whole story.

I want people to care about our firefighters, because every day they're on the frontline, putting their lives at risk for them. I've spoken to many of the firefighters who were at the Grenfell Tower fire of 2017, all of them scarred for life. I've seen things that I am still haunted by years later. The mental impact of our work and post-traumatic stress disorder (PTSD) is present throughout the Fire Service and we need to recognise that firefighters put themselves on the line every day and I don't want that to be for nothing. I think the first step is to humanise us, to take off the fire gear and the breathing apparatus masks and show the people underneath, warts and all – the tears, yes, but the fun and the laughter too.

Because some days you're crawling on your hands and knees, a canopy of flame blossoming on the ceiling above you, the steam and smoke clouding your vision; the roar of the fire and the flow of pressurised air in your breathing apparatus mask, like you're deep underwater. Nine hundred degrees Celsius igniting paint on doors and frames, popping and cracking plastered walls and ceilings and lightbulbs exploding from the heat. Every cell in your body instinctively trying to persuade you that you shouldn't be there.

Other days you're watching Phil see how many marsh-mallows he can fit in one cheek.

The simple truth is I've spent so much of my career laughing, because as with any job where the stakes are so high, it's a coping mechanism, an attempt to remain human in response to so much that is horrifying. That's not to say that we ever take our job lightly, or that we're indifferent to the tragedy surrounding us. But that laughter is an essential pressure release, as most people operating in life-or-death jobs will attest. A way to recalibrate the brain and to find humanity with those around you who share the pressure and the stress and those sights that we can't forget. But mainly I think there's just something fundamentally fascinating about the only people running *into* a burning building. Firefighters are just wired differently. It's a job of extremes – sitting around, waiting for something to happen. And then something *really* happens. I've been lucky enough to see the best in people when the worst is happening. I've seen extraordinary bravery, teamwork and compassion. I've seen the strength in people when they're pushed to the very edge. I wouldn't swap it for any other job in the world.

Once, when I was a kid, my mum asked me what I wanted to be when I grew up and I proudly answered, 'A firefighter.'

Mum laughed. 'Well, then you'll have to choose one or the other, because you can't do both – firefighters never grow up.'

It's only now, with twenty-five years of service under my belt, that I feel like I can fully explain why.

2

How Fires Start

Fire. Arguably mankind's most important discovery. Knowledge from the gods. The rapid oxidisation of a material in an exothermic chemical process known as combustion.[1] However you want to describe it, human beings are obsessed with it. Seriously. When have you ever been near an open fire and someone goes 'Oh, I hate looking at fire!' It's what allowed our ancestors to keep those animals in the dark away from us and for us to become modern humans. We love it. In summer barbecues, in winter bonfires. And for most of my adult life, it's been my job to get rid of it. But oddly, one of my most vivid memories is of a fire I started.

Like all young boys, I loved flames. Nothing entertained me more than getting a big box of pink-tipped Swan Vesta matches, striking one and then popping the lit end inside. The brief whoosh of fire and smoke was nicknamed 'The Genie' by the kids round our way and it delivered an efficient buzz for a ten-year-old kid

---

1 Thank you, Wikipedia.

waiting for the bus home from school.[2]

For many years of my young life I was even actively encouraged to start fires with the Scouts. A speciality of mine was collecting a nice pile of kindling before rubbing two bits of wood together in order to create a fire – essential should I be left stranded in the wilderness with nothing but a packet of crisps and some Opal Fruits.

This particular time it was summer and I was messing around with some mates in a cornfield near our school. Everything was bone-dry and for some reason I decided to flick a lit match into the highly flammable crop. At first, I didn't think anything of it, but minutes later, I noticed a thin curlicue of smoke drifting into the sky. *That's weird*, I thought. And having stepped towards it, a gust of wind seemed to sweep overhead. *Whoosh!* The ground in front of me was suddenly ablaze and the flames were spreading outwards, terrifyingly quickly. I heard someone shout: *Run!* In a flash, we were all legging it as far away as possible.

My lungs wheezed from the effort, the muscles in my calves and thighs burned too. But one motivational sentence played over and over in my head as I sprinted: *Shit, shit, shit! I am in so much trouble.*

It's funny the things that stick in the brain during an event of that kind. As the whole field went up behind us, I noticed that one of the lads I was fleeing with was

---

2 Parents take note: you wouldn't believe the amount of times I've attended an incident where a house has gone up in smoke because one of the children living inside had decided to set fire to a corner of his duvet, 'just to see what might happen'. Within minutes, that bedroom and with it, all those cool toys, computer tech, books and posters are destroyed.

the school's 100 metres champion, a real Usain Bolt-in-the-making, and for the first few 100 metres or so, he was nothing but a dot in the field ahead. By the time we had covered about a kilometre, I'd not only caught up, but I'd shown him my heels and the look on his face was a picture.

'What?! How the hell are you faster than me, Leigh?' he shouted as I left him for dust.

'Because my dad's a firefighter,' I yelled back. 'And he's on duty today.'

By the time I'd burst through the front door to our house, the smoke from my little accident was choking the town. Then I heard the fire engines. I knew Dad would be sitting in one of them, dressed in his fire gear, ready to go. And I knew I'd hear all about the incident when he got home for his dinner later that night. I stressed about how I was going to deliver the perfect look of innocence as he regaled me with the finer details. I hadn't really wanted to start a fire. I'd been stupid for sure, but it wasn't a malicious act. I rehearsed a potential defence: *In many ways, with so much time spent with the Scouts, I'd almost been primed for that very moment, Your Honour.* But I knew Dad wouldn't quite see it that way, so when he came home ranting and raving over dinner about some 'little shits' that had razed the local cornfield to ash, I chewed my chips and kept schtum. He still doesn't know to this day.[3]

---

3 Dad, this was entirely made up by the publisher to add some excitement to the chapter. Honest.

★

At this point, I should probably do a very quick science lesson. One of the first things every recruit has to endure as they work towards becoming a competent and experienced firefighter is a bombardment of information on the anatomy of a blaze. How it starts, how it transforms from a small, smouldering burn into a raging inferno. And how you kill it. In an early class, possibly the first on the itinerary, the newbie will learn about the 'Triangle of Fire', an equation that details the three components needed to trigger an emergency call. In no particular order these are (a) oxygen, (b) fuel and (c) a heat source. Sure, there are all sorts of additional factors that can determine the intensity of the fire, such as the type of fuel and its quantity, but oxygen + fuel + heat = the basic formula.[4]

But strangely, the instructors at training school rarely inform the men and women under their tutelage that there is a fourth, unspoken component that can kick-start a blaze; one that is very obviously present in that cornfield and which, technically, reworks the Triangle of Fire into a square. And that added extra is sheer, unblinking human stupidity. Whether it's a bloke pouring a can of petrol onto his shed and throwing in a light 'to

---

4 Once these key bits of intelligence have been absorbed, a trainee is then imparted with a level of knowledge reserved for the brain trust on *The Chase*, such as the process of pyrolysis, which, according to the *Encyclopedia Britannica* is 'the chemical decomposition of organic (carbon-based) materials through the application of heat'. (Don't yawn, you'll thank me when it comes up in a pub quiz.)

see what would happen', or the countless people who think that a night at the pub + late night TV + a cheeky last cigarette is a good combination. You won't be too shocked to learn that it's something I get to experience now on a regular basis.

It seems obvious looking back that I was always going to be a firefighter. I was surrounded by firefighters from the minute my parents were able to show me off to their friends and family. My dad, Reg, was in the job, as was my grandad on my mum's side, Ron, who overcame a near-death incident in the North Atlantic when the Royal Navy support ship he was serving on during World War II lost engine power and drifted into the Arctic Ocean. The British armed forces, presuming the vessel and crew had been wiped out by a German U-boat attack, soon called off their search. But after weeks without radio contact, during which time the ship's supplies of food and water had dwindled away to nothing, the crew was discovered off the coast of Greenland, huddled together in −18°C temperatures. Most of them were violently ill with dysentery. After that little experience, dousing blazes and saving cats from trees probably felt like a stroll through the park.

And the job had a fair amount of kudos back in the day. It must have done because once my dad had started dating Mum, he had taken a keen interest in what his future father-in-law was up to. I'm not surprised. Firefighters were brave and selfless. They saved lives, rescued cats from trees and cut jug-eared kids from metal railing fences. *Girls loved them.* And once Dad, at that point a lorry driver, had seen a fire engine racing past him as he unloaded his flatbed at the roadside one day, he experienced a life-altering epiphany: *he was going to join the Fire Brigade.*

Then there was my uncle, Trevor, who was also in the Service. Sadly, he died before I ever got the chance to know him properly, though there was always a picture of him on the family mantelpiece, at the top of a tall Fire Service ladder, in a shiny black cork fire helmet. By the time I got to school age, my grandad had long retired too, but he was always telling stories of his against-the-odds endeavours.

Growing up, the men in my family smelt of smoke. That's just how it was. As a kid, I was obsessed with anything fast-moving, loud and shiny, especially the bright red fire engines. I loved the bold colours, the flashing lights and the noisy sirens. I dreamt of sliding down one of those famous shiny old poles, which were featured in most fire stations in those days. I too was going to be a firefighter and save lives, rescue cats from trees and cut jug-eared kids from metal railing fences.

Growing up, my favourite moments were when I was taken to the station for an hour or two as a treat. Mum wasn't working then and sometimes, if my sister and I had been well behaved, she'd take us in to see Dad on duty. I loved messing around with his mates and the earliest memories I have of being around firemen, which is what they were called in the 1970s, always engendered a sense of safety and security. I'd climb in and out of the engines and slide down the steel pole that linked a dormitory to the appliance (fire engine) bay downstairs; I was fussed over by a team of big, burly blokes, all of them soft, caring and understanding; each of them another father figure to hang about with. It left a big impression on me. There was also a more pressing reason for those visits too. As a kid, I had really bad asthma. One way to clear my heaving lungs from pollens and allergens was to fix a breathing apparatus mask over my face, the type found in fire stations across the country. Dad would sit me on the back of the appliance and the cool, filtered air would calm my laboured wheezing.

Nothing was more exciting than those new-term, introductory classes in school, when all the kids in the room were asked about what their parents did for a living. Most of the time, the answers were predictably boring. But once my turn arrived, I made sure to enjoy the moment.

I stood up, and proudly said, 'My dad's a fireman.'

A gasp of excitement would travel around the circle of kids sitting crossed-legged on the floor and I loved it. Even the teachers were impressed. Firefighters were heroes. *Everybody knew it.* Certainly, in my eyes, Dad was. I always thought, *He's brave, he's fearless and courageous.* But what really added to my street cred was being able to show my mates around Dad's workplace during the summer holidays, or getting the nod to ride shotgun in the engine (while it was still parked in the station, of course). I suppose in a way I'd been conditioned. Like most kids, I believed if my dad could do it, there was no reason why I couldn't be brave, fearless and courageous too. Some people wanted to fly to the moon, win court cases or cut down trees for a living, I wanted to put out fires.

★

Of course, the idea of mortality never really struck me back then. Now that I'm an established firefighter, with kids of my own, it's very different but then it was simple: Dad was a hero. He pulled terrified families from burning buildings, cut injured drivers from cars and even saved some people unlucky enough to fall through the ice in our local lake one January. But as a little kid, not once did I think, *He might not come home today.* Dad hadn't wanted to give that impression either. But as I grew up, the reality slowly dawned that, OK, what he was doing was risky and the fact that he would come home in the evening for cuddles and dinner wasn't 100 per cent guaranteed.

It had helped that the conversations around the dinner table were fairly on the surface. My parents, quite rightly, weren't big on discussing the grislier details of a fatal car accident over the shepherd's pie. But as I grew older and became more naturally inquisitive, more and more truths about the work of the Fire Service were imparted upon me until eventually in my teens I was given fuller briefings on just how gruesome it could be. With hindsight, as a father myself now, I reckon he was preparing me. Dad wanted me to know that a life in the Fire Brigade wasn't all excitement and derring-do. There was plenty of blood and guts and tears to go with those high-speed journeys in a shiny red truck, its blue lights spinning.

Dad made sure to balance out the goriness in his stories though. More than anything, life as a firefighter sounded fun – *funny*. I heard about the practical jokes in the mess (dining) room and how certain watch members were forever being stitched up. Then there were those weird and wonderful run-ins with the public. More often than not, the family was entertained by Dad's stories when he returned home from work, rather than horrified. But what it meant was to a certain extent danger was normalised for me as a teenager. Don't get me wrong, though I wasn't fearful, I could hardly be described as a head case. Rather, my path had been set. The reality of the firefighting life felt intriguing. There was mystery and risk. And as I became older and I could understand the emotions and details of the job, thanks to Dad's increasingly graphic stories, the idea of following in his footsteps flipped from being a childish fantasy into a serious career option. I suppose the same thing happened to kids whose parents had served in the military. And like those boys and girls, I had grown up with a keen sense of discipline. I loved the idea of working to serious schedules and procedures; I was good with time keeping and structure. In fact, having recognised my ambitions to join the Fire Brigade, Dad encouraged me to sign up with the Air Cadets when I was in my teens.

'It'll be fun,' he said. 'You'll get to go flying.'

I'd also learn to appreciate the value of a keenly polished pair of shoes and a neatly pressed shirt, because taking care of your appearance – an early development phase when learning attention to detail – was very important.

Getting into the job was a grind though. Like most teenagers, I worked through all sorts of gigs to earn money. I served customers in a shop for a while. A little while later I became a salesperson and I hated every minute of it. The work was predictable and boring. But then, at the age of eighteen, the Fire Service in my county went on an aggressive recruitment drive. *And I wanted in.* But there was no easy ticket to success and Dad of all people told me I was too young to join.

'You've just turned eighteen,' he said. 'Give it some time.'

I didn't listen and filled out the forms anyway. To the surprise of no one, my application was rejected. It was rejected again at the ages of nineteen and twenty too.

Bloody hell, I thought. *Is this it? Am I not even going to get a shot at training?*

Dad knew my time would come eventually. He kept reassuring me whenever I grumbled about my circumstances and the hard knocks.

'It's important that you get yourself some life experience,' he advised. 'That's why they keep pushing you back. They'll call you at some point.'

I wasn't so sure and I'd already started to do well as a welding supplies salesman, promising myself that if, by the age of twenty-one I hadn't been taken in, I'd give up on the idea of joining the Fire Service altogether. Not that I was overly happy with my self-imposed deadline. My boss at the welding supplies company had sensed that my heart wasn't in sales, almost from the minute I'd joined with him, but I hadn't wanted to be brutally honest during my job interview in case he binned me off on the spot. And then, out of nowhere, the Fire Service's recruitment office called – another trainee spot had opened up. *Would I be interested?* I didn't need to pause for thought, I was out of the door of the welding supplies company and readying myself for a life of adventure.

3

Into the Frying Pan

Training school was a gruelling seventeen weeks of seemingly endless back-to-back drills. Ladders, pumping. More
ladders, more pumping. Cutting equipment techniques
and swathes of breathing apparatus wears. Repeated again
and again. They're prepping you with the fundamentals,
so you're not a total liability in your first few weeks and
months on station and there hasn't been a week that's
gone by when I haven't been grateful for the grounding
it gave me.

Arriving at an incident, you never quite know what
you're going to find. That's as true when you arrive
with the blue lights flashing as the more low-wattage
moments. And especially true a few years ago when
there was a government initiative subsidised with Fire &
Rescue services to encourage the entire nation to have
a working smoke alarm on every floor of their property.
Any household could call up their local Fire Service to
request these alarms. This formed part of a home safety
visit, during which the attending crew assessed safety
routines and general lifestyle around the home. We'd also
ensure there were no overloaded plug sockets and that

the visible wiring for all electrical appliances was in good nick. As a parting gift, we'd advise how to improve fire safety before setting up as many box-fresh smoke alarms as we considered necessary – you know, the kind that always bleep annoyingly whenever the battery is about to run out.

Literally anyone could request these visits. One afternoon, I was part of a two-man team asked to attend a suburban home in our fire-ground.[1] The door was opened by a middle-aged woman whose smile became a rictus grin when she saw who we were.

'Oh hello, gentlemen,' she said, obviously taken aback. 'That's today, is it?'

There's a lot you can tell about a person within a few seconds of crossing their threshold and firefighters have a knack for assessing a situation, given we're in and out of people's homes all the time. In other words, we're super observant! In this case, I suspected the woman lived alone. Or at least there was no evidence that a man was living there anyway. No male shoes or coats by the front door; I didn't see any repeated male figures in the photos. Meanwhile, the owner seemed very officious. In her sharp skirt, blouse and severe ponytail, she carried a grave look about her and after a brief chat about her general fire safety concerns, she guided us around the house.[2]

Having shown us the second floor, the homeowner – let's call her 'Ms X' for the purposes of this story – pointed

---

1 Professional speak for the area on which our station primarily attends 999 calls.

2 Her main concern being 'I don't really want my house to burn down.'

22

to an annexe area. 'Oh, did I mention that I usually work from home?' she said. 'That's my office.'

I peeked inside to check for any faulty light fittings, or perhaps an overloaded electrical socket. The 'office' turned out to be a dimly lit room, with dark painted wooden panels and racks around the walls equipped with the devices you might recognise from a particularly brutal episode of *Game of Thrones*. Whips, handcuffs and what can only be described as 'miscellaneous blunt instruments' dangled from one rack. All sorts of leather outfits and uniforms had been stored in a corner.

Bloody hell, I thought. *Fair play to her.*

Despite my attempts to project a liberal, non-judgemental attitude, an awkward silence descended. This was punctured by the rattle of chains and a muffled sound from somewhere in the gloom. When I looked harder, I saw a man, his arms tied together above his head. Shoved in a corner and chained to a ring that was affixed to the wall, he was squeezed into what looked like a painfully tight, shiny rubber suit, which the internet reliably informs me was a PVC 'gimp' suit.[3] His PVC onesie was fixed with an assortment of zippers, one of which was positioned in a very intimate place. The look was offset by a ball gag.

Raising a hand, the gimp waved cheerily. A muffled, garbled noise seemed to say, 'Hello' though I cannot be certain. Either way, he didn't seem too unhappy to be there.

Ms X, having seen what we'd seen, tried to normalise

---

3 Which, just so you know, would go up like a bonfire.

the situation.[4] 'Oh don't worry about him,' she said, coyly. 'That's Sebastian. And Sebastian's been a *very* naughty boy!'

My colleague and I fixed the smoke alarms happily, taking care not to upset Madame X on our way out.

There are the times we've been called in for even more intimate reasons. Everyone who's ever had to remove their wedding ring knows that fingers swell through heat, medical conditions, or even too many Scotch eggs and as a result, any worn, attached rings then bite into the skin. As any doctor will tell you, this only exacerbates the problem. Once the finger has started to swell and throb, the tightness increases, causing the digit to become even more engorged. Blood pools around either side of the band, making it impossible to shift the ring up or down and the only way to free it is to slice away with a small thumb-wheel cutter, which carries a serrated, circular blade. Slowly, but surely, by working the wheel, it's possible to detach the jewellery from the finger.

Just about every fire station in the UK is equipped with one of these simple yet very effective wheels. The police know about them, the Ambulance services too, so when anyone staggers onto their premises looking to free their podgy digits, they're usually sent our way. On this one particular occasion, the local A&E department put a call in to our service: apparently their latest victim was in a bad way and unable to move. When the officer-in-charge that day arrived at the hospital in

---

4 Actually, let's call her 'Madame X'.

an appliance, plus five firefighters, he was introduced to the triage nurse on duty.

'Someone has turned up with an object stuck on their person,' she announced, shyly. 'We didn't have an idea how to get it off, so we called you . . .'

Something was off. The nurse was trying desperately not to smirk. It was only when the officer entered the treatment cubicle and was introduced to the patient, a middle-aged male who looked very sheepish, that the awful truth was revealed: no rings were visible on his fingers.

'So, what are we looking at here, sir?'

The nurse lifted the sheet and pointed downwards.

'It's under here . . .'

When the cover was pulled back, a definitely not-safe-for-work image was revealed: the poor bloke was stiff as a board, his painfully aroused member held erect by a metal 'cock ring'.[5] Having heard the gadget's marketing assurances that a marital aid of this kind encourages a longer, harder erection, the smooth steel toy had been slipped on. But it must have been too tight and sliding it off was now impossible because, well . . . it was doing its job. Interestingly, rather than being embarrassed, he seemed relatively proud and the 'situation' was only inflamed further by five inquisitive firefighters crowding in to take a look, in preparation for a delicate release.[6] Although no selfies were taken, apparently the ring was

---

5 Please don't Google it at work if you don't know.

6 Safety tip: if you're about to put a bit of your body somewhere metal, just ask yourself what might possibly go wrong. If one of the thoughts involves flashing blue lights then that's probably a sign.

not disposed of at the hospital. Firefighters are proud individuals. Proud of the jobs we do. Rumour has it the shiny toy made its way back to a fire station somewhere and was painstakingly reassembled as a constant reminder of a job well done.

Though there wasn't exactly a specific unit of training for gimps and willy rings, I like to think our calm-under-pressure and impeccable professional demeanour in these circumstances would have done our instructors from all those years ago proud.

I had known that it was going to be tough joining the Fire Service after my dad but I wasn't prepared for just how tough. From the very first minute of my very first day at training school, I was comically thrashed. This was mainly on the basis that my dad was an established fire-fighter with twenty years' experience so it was expected, rightly or wrongly, that I would be as good as, if not leaner and meaner than him. They knew full well that their actions would make their way back to Dad when I groaned about it all. At times it was genuinely hard to figure out whether they were aiming to raise a laugh (they did), or settle some ancient pranking scores as a result.

The site of our greatest personal battles was the drill yard – an area where we gathered daily for inspections, equipment testing and operational scenario drills. The drill yard was regarded as the ultimate testing ground for every 'recruit' (the Fire Service's term for a trainee). They knew we needed to hit the ground running, so they worked us *hard*, reckoning that drilling as much as possible into our muscle memory was the best way to free up space in the brain to respond to the situation. However, what that meant, was if you found something difficult, you found it difficult *a lot*.

Weekly written tests were conducted every Monday morning and those recruits unable to match the high standards set by the Fire Service were soon told to empty their lockers. A number of my fellow recruits assumed my progression would be assured, owing to Dad's hefty reputation within the upper echelons of the Service, but that wasn't to be the case. In fact, it turned out to be the opposite and at the end of week one, my name was called out over the training centre's tannoy system. I was told to empty my locker and present myself at the training commandant's office in full dress uniform – the smartest uniform we wear, comprising bulled shoes, trousers, shirt and tie, epaulets, jacket and cap.

'That doesn't sound too good,' one recruit colleague noted darkly.

I thought of having to tell my family that I was out after just one week.

'So, how do you think you've done in your first week, Firefighter Hosy-Pickett?' asked the training comman-dant, opening a case file with my name on it. He was flanked by two other training school sub-officers. The scene felt incredibly formal.

'Well, it's my first week, so . . .'

'Actually, don't bother answering,' he snapped. 'Let's see for ourselves, shall we?'

The atmosphere crackled as he read silently for a couple of minutes.

'Hmm, not very good at pump operating, not good with ladders, or heights, poor exam results . . .' said the commandant. 'Are you sure you want to take this job on? More importantly, do you even have the capacity to do it?'

Suddenly my career, *my dream*, seemed to be in tatters; I could feel my eyes brimming with tears.[7] Then he burst into fits of laughter.

'I can't do this anymore,' he snorted. '*How's your dad?*'

I glanced across at the faces in the room. *It had been a wind-up.* They were all smirking. In that moment I hated every single one of them, but I'd been given an early insight into the special kind of humour located at the heart of the Fire Brigade. I learned that my progression in the role would be booby-trapped with this sort of thing.

But that was only a small part of what I was learning. During those seventeen weeks of firefighter training school, our time was broken down into four components. The first phase: twelve weeks focused on pumps and ladders, where everyone was expected to master the kind of skills needed to work safely and effectively on a firecall. The second phase, which lasted five weeks: week one and two educated every recruit in the safe and proficient use of hydraulic rescue equipment, which was required to deal with road traffic collisions.[8] Week

---

7 I half-expected him to say, 'Firefighter has a history of lighting fires in corn fields.'

8 The term 'traffic accident' was banned as a definition some time ago. Someone escaped a custodial sentence after proving that the collision they caused was merely an accident, as the prosecution described it. They got off by proving that no one could be responsible for an 'accident'.

three and four was a fortnight of Breathing Apparatus (BA) training, and the final week dealt with the type of fire-related events so beloved by Hollywood directors. Those being flashovers, and backdrafts – a ferocious, roaring burst of flame that took place when fresh air was re-introduced into a once-burning room. Having sucked all the oxygen from that space, a blaze could be reinvigorated by a fresh source from an opened door or window, and this was a reaction to be feared.[9]

Over the course of those four months or so, I learned that fire was a temperamental animal – *a living thing*. Sea captains and navy crew would talk about how the sea was alive, how the tides and waves seemed to have a schizophrenic personality. Sometimes the ocean could be kind, even benign. On other occasions it would pitch and yaw with an unpredictable fury, destroying everything in its path. Fire was no different. It was an animal, a monster, untamed. It didn't care for you, or your life; it couldn't give a shit about your hopes and dreams, your fears, or plans for the weekend. I was taught that if I couldn't control it, it would turn round and bite me. If I didn't respect it, the flames would eat me up like some nightmarish beast. But if I treated it right, sometimes it might just give me a little love, or at least there could be mutual respect.

Strange as that may sound, I was taught there would be situations where it was smart to allow a fire to burn within the same room I was in. When searching for a person, or persons trapped somewhere in a building, it

---

9 May I refer you to that triangle of fire again.

was important to make the most of any emitting light coming from it in order to locate them, even if that light came from a burning sofa. On other occasions, I was taught how the upsides of putting out a fire could be outweighed by the downsides. For example, aiming water at a raging blaze always created a massive plume of steam.[10] This could cause some serious damage to anyone trapped in its path. In those moments of chaos, a firefighter could find themselves suddenly blinded in situations where it was imperative to keep an eye on the air gauges attached to their breathing apparatus (they help keep a firefighter alive after all). All this give and take resembled a conflict between monster and man and at times I'd almost begin a conversation with the burn around me.

OK, I respect you, I'd think. *I'm going see what you're doing and check if you're going to get worse.* Or, *If I leave you alone, will you allow me to see what's going on here? If so, I'll allow you to carry on burning because it's what you want to do. If not, I'm putting you out, mate . . .*

The harsh lessons associated with fire management were scary, but they weren't as scary as those moments where I'd screwed up in front of my squad mates and peers. With every blunder, a sub-officer – the person responsible for turning a probationer from a wannabe know-nothing into a fully-fledged, life-saving superhero

---

10 At average atmospheric pressure, the expansion ratio between water in its liquid form and steam is 1:1,700. This means that under ideal conditions, one part of liquid water expands to 1,700 times the volume as steam when boiled. Not great in the confines of a domestic property.

– made it absolutely clear how high the standards were and that I was nowhere close yet. One task expected of everyone in training was the efficient execution of 'running out and making hose up', a routine in which the recruits would roll out and then 'under run' the hose used during drills, before rolling it up and stowing it away.[11] It was bread-and-butter stuff for everyone in the job, really. But I soon discovered there was a real art to nailing the procedure successfully and failing to do so had a number of consequences: 1) A poorly rolled hose would flare out, or 'cone' in the middle, making it very difficult to store back on the appliance; 2) A coned hose was also a complete nightmare to roll out again when it was required on a shout where speed was everything. And 3) It looked shit. In much the same way that the Royal Marines Commandos were expected to keep their kit and weapon dry, so a member of the Fire Service was expected to show attention to detail when putting their respective equipment away – a poorly rolled hose was a telltale sign of an unthinking firefighter.

I knew all of this because I'd seen it countless times as a kid when I was taken to the station to watch Dad and his watch mates perform the same drills over and over. When they did it, it seemed effortless, as if they

---

11 'Under run' was a term we used for removing the water from a hose. The hose was first laid out flat. You then step in around two metres from the branch, or nozzle, picking up the hose and placing it on your shoulder, feeding it as you walk its length to the other end. Gravity and the angle of the hose then allowed any residual water inside to pour out from the coupling. After that was done, you'd roll it up. Sounds easy, doesn't it? It wasn't!

didn't have to think about it at all. It was like watching a top-level sports person in the zone. I knew why it was important too. As I'd grown older, and learned more and more about the job, the importance of drills was hammered into me. My dad certainly understood that training made the job of fighting real fires that much easier because muscle memory was key to being safe. It meant that you were able to have greater awareness of the risks around you at an incident. The real world was always going to be very different to the training ground. Sure, when pulling up to a house blaze, the nearest fire hydrant might have been positioned differently to the one on the drill ground; the fire engine might have parked at a slightly different angle to the training appliance in place at the station. But through repeated practice, the fundamentals of what had to be done on the job eventually became second nature. That's because the skills required to succeed were sharpened over and over – and then over and over again. And it didn't end with training either. Once passed out of the seventeen-week course, a fully-fledged member of the Fire Service would then be tasked with drills on a near-daily or nightly basis. The constant repetition gave me that muscle memory in situations where instinct was everything, but in that moment, it seemed never-ending.

Making hose up proved my nemesis in those first few weeks of the pumps and ladders training phase. My first attempt looked like an upended bowl of spaghetti, my second like the top of a Mr Whippy ice cream on a really hot day. God, I was bad at it, and a sub-officer had spotted my weakness. He also knew Dad really well, which meant that I could expect to receive an extra serving of detailed critiques on my technique and he dished it out with a smug grin on his face. The routine was always the same. I'd watch, sadly, as my hose sagged and drooped into a weird cone shape, waiting for the inevitable call for the recruits to down tools. And then the humbling would begin.

'Rest!' shouted the sub-officer, which was a term used to bring training to a halt so a mistake could be corrected.

I saw his shadow looming over my hose.

'What the bloody hell is that, Pickett?' he said.

The temptation to point out that it was a hose was hard to control.[12]

'Don't answer that, I know what it bloody well is!' he snapped. 'I mean, what have you done with it?'

My heart sank. I was all out of excuses and the consequences of my actions would be both painful and public.

'Do it again,' said the sub-officer.

Again?

'Again.'

So, I huffed and puffed, rolling, under running and re-rolling, only to be told that my attempts were 'pathetic', not that it needed pointing out. I could feel the eyes of my training squad burning into me. I knew they were

---

12 My dad once told me of a similar situation when he was invited to a formal meeting after a senior probational officer arrived at his station to check in on him. Having sat down, Dad was asked how he'd been finding the station. 'Well, sir,' he replied, 'I come out of my house and turn left. At the junction, I turn right. At the next junction, I turn left and the station is around 300 yards up, on the left.' The senior officer hit the roof. And the lesson? Being a smart-arse was not a good idea.

all thinking exactly the same thing: *I'm so glad his dad's in the Fire Service and not mine.*

'You should know better,' continued the sub-officer, having first pulled me up on some mistake or other. 'Your father's been in the job long enough . . .'

When I got home that night and spoke to my dad, I surprised myself with how annoyed I was by it. The snarky comments had finally got to me: 'It doesn't matter what I do, it's never good enough because I'm the son of a firefighter. It's like they think I grew up rolling hoses or something,' I moaned.

Dad just laughed. 'Don't take it personally!' he said. 'They're going home tonight and they know that you'll be telling me and they'll know that I'll be laughing. It's all a game, you've just got to learn how to play it.'

But that night, as I finally slipped into a restless sleep, the last thing I pictured was a long line of perfectly rolled hoses.

4

Out of the Frying Pan

Training was repetitive for a reason. The Service knew that there was so much they could never prepare us for that they *really* wanted to make sure we knew what we were doing with everything else. A good example of this was a blue-light call in the early hours a few years ago. My crew had been despatched to a less affluent part of town and when we arrived at the building, thick black smoke was billowing away from every crack and gap in the windows and doors. By the look of things the blaze inside was a beast and as the designated first firefighter in, I'd been rigged into my breathing apparatus and all the equipment required to deal with a serious incident, part of which included a 'thermal imaging camera' (TIC). This incredible piece of kit lets us see through thick blankets of smoke – essential when trying to locate missing people. Once I'd breached the front door and entered, a strange sight struck me. The place was a menagerie of vegetation. Plant tendrils with broad, serrated leaves had grown to the ceiling and the floor space was arranged with what looked like large, potted trees.

Bloody hell! Is this Alan Titchmarsh's place? I wondered.

If it was, he'd developed an interesting sideline in high times. With my breathing apparatus on, it was impossible to detect any odour. But having spotted the floodlights positioned at one end of the room, some of them ablaze, the enormity of what I'd walked into began to dawn on me.

'Fucking hell, it's a light . . .' I said out loud, forgetting my radio was live and transmitting, as they always were.

'Of course it's alight,' snapped my governor on the other end of the comms, 'that's why you're in there! Put some water on it.'

'No, guv. It's a *light* – a floodlight. There's seven or eight of them and we're stood among a massive cannabis crop – Snoop Dogg's by the looks of it.'

Having delivered instructions to any eyewitnesses standing outside not to inhale – unless they wanted a *really* good night's kip – we extinguished the blaze and surveyed the wreckage of a one-time family-sized home for the fire's exact cause. Once I'd arrived at the electric meter, the main power source for the building, Point C of the Triangle of Fire wasn't too hard to locate. The heat source was found at the armoured cable, the type that usually connected a house, or flat, to the National Grid. An improvised electric meter bypass was also visible. At first glance this was a primitive extension lead, but it turned out this device had been attached to an exposed and very live part of armoured cable. More alarming though was the series of metal crocodile clips directly attached to the mains – talk about ballsy![1]

---

[1] Safety tip: unless you're a qualified electrician, do not mess around with electricity. In the same way if you're not a qualified lion tamer don't mess about with lions.

I immediately recognised another setup close-by – a booby trap designed to fry any rival gangs or organised dealers hoping to raid a lucrative harvest. In fact, improvised security systems of that kind were also found at pirate radio stations. In hideouts of that nature, the aerials on the top of a high-rise building were usually rigged up as a deterrent for anyone thinking of tearing them down, such as the aforementioned gangs or a busybody neighbour. But like this weed factory, the antennas usually ended up in a pile of ashes.

Still, the selfishness and stupidity always amazed me. The individuals running this particular herbal warehouse hadn't stopped to consider the safety of the people working to save them and their property. Also, a little foresight might have helped to prevent the meltdown in the first place: 'Hold on a minute, if we rig this hotwired security system up and we have a fire in the building, those poor firefighters are going to get the shock of their lives. Let's have a rethink . . .' Nor did they consider the fact that such a volatile energy source connection would wreak so much havoc in a building packed with a hell of a lot of flammable material.

There's every chance they might have been stoned though.

That day, I was grateful, yet again, to the teachers who gave me the foundations to survive that sort of scenario at all.

Back at the training ground, Dad's pep talk had been a turning point and something just clicked. I knuckled down, learned to take their feedback, also sometimes known as piss taking, on the chin and from that point on I stopped seeing the jabs as unnecessarily cruel. Instead there was an acceptance that my dad's reputation was a cross I'd have to bear from time to time and it was up to me to prove that I was as good as him. However, in order to do so, I'd have to prove I was better than everyone else around me.

One of the most important lessons instilled into the new recruit involved locker maintenance. In the same way it was considered reckless if a soldier ignored duty of care for their weapon, a firefighter would be regarded as less than the full ticket if they were to leave their locker unlocked, but for very different reasons. Nothing would have been stolen (there's little petty crime at a fire station). No one was likely to die because of an unguarded locker (it's an issue of personal care rather than health and safety). But the guilty party would always get a soaking, courtesy of a half-filled rubber wellie folded inside (these days, the ones we wear are leather). The trick was simple: by wedging the water-filled boot on the top shelf of a locker it created an effective booby trap device that exploded over the victim as soon as they opened the door. I've watched probationers half-open their locker and realise too late that they've been pranked. They're able to see their painful fate unfold in slow motion but taking evasive action is impossible – the only way out is to absorb the soaking as quickly as possible. There's a very simple reason behind this soggy memory aid – you need to trust that everyone is keeping on top of the details and keeping equipment in the very best condition. At any one time you could be relying on something someone else packed, or maintained. It starts with your own locker. Hence the wet wellie.

Getting soaked during the pumps and ladders stretch of training was something we all got used to. One of the more regularly executed training scenarios was called a 'composite drill', a standard session comprising ladder pitches, pumping and hose management. This involved twelve firefighters and two crews of six (six being the maximum number of people able to fit onto one appliance). To start things off, we'd all stand in a line where we were given numbers. The officer-in-charge for the purpose of the exercise was Number One. Number Two was the driver and pump operator. And if you were numbers three, four, five and six, you were managing hose or going up the ladder with a long line, which was used to haul aloft the delivery hose and branch, plus other pieces of equipment, if required.[2]

Once the hose had been fixed into position, whoever was in charge of the branch was effectively transformed into a sniper, which could be very effective when positioned at a very high vantage point, and able to fire a huge volume of water from a 70mm hose branch. The blast was powerful enough to help calm the flames on a blazing inferno and there were many stories of officers on this detail, drenching the squad below with a weapons-grade super-soaker. Elsewhere, it was widely considered that the worst position in the drill was to be the pump operator, where it required a recruit to hold their position throughout, come hell or high water. With nowhere to

---

2 We call a rope a line – it's a naval thing.

run to and nowhere to hide, it was inevitable that the poor sod on that detail would receive a soaking. Granted, they had the power to end such shenanigans by shutting off the pump, but the bollocking from a training officer for doing so was far worse than the drenching itself, so it never happened. But the pasting was taken with a smile. If only because the roles were always switched around after and the pump operator could exact a revenge that was sweet, wet and cold – very cold, especially if the training was taking place in January!

The joking soon stopped once we'd been ushered into the next training phase: the grisly business of what is now called the Road Traffic Collision course, a two-week process where we learned how to cut the injured from concertinaed cars and lorries, and the best methods for releasing bodies from tangled, multi-car, motorway pile-ups. This module was not for the faint-hearted and any thoughts on just how unpleasant our work was set to be were soon amplified by an introductory session with an individual I'll affectionately refer to here as 'Doctor Death' – an experienced officer who took his duty to impress upon us the mechanics of flesh, blood and bone and how it reacted to collisions with another object when moving ninety miles per hour very seriously. Everyone on my squad had heard that these lessons were bordering on the gruesome – it was part of Fire Service folklore. We all steeled our stomachs accordingly.

Much of this reputation was a result of the 'Folder of Blood' – a portfolio of educational images taken from past car incidents. There were hundreds of them and each image was a snapshot of death. Headless victims slumped over steering wheels, corpses hanging from windows, people squashed like bugs on the back seat.[3] Each photograph had a story attached to it and there was a practical cause of death for each. Some of them were obvious: a head had been ripped clean off and this was an injury not considered compatible with life. Others were not so obvious. For example, when a car collided with another vehicle at speed, the occupants often ricocheted around inside the vehicle, even if they'd been wearing their seat belts. In those incidents, the internal organs are shaken around at a high velocity. Aortas are severed, the heart and lungs can be torn or punctured. Imagine shaking up a tin of plum tomatoes for a few seconds. That's what can happen to the human body when smashing into an immovable object at ninety miles per hour.[4]

Doctor Death's macabre portfolio was a warning of things to come. In many ways we were being toughened up for the unpleasant sights awaiting us when in the line of duty. During lectures, he would open up his folder, then pass his gory scrapbook around the class with a cheery invitation to take a look.

'Tuck in,' he'd say, aware that we were about to be traumatised, albeit in a very controlled sense.

---

3 If you're not getting the deliberately not-so-subtle messaging at play here, let me spell it out for you: don't be a dick, drive carefully and never break the speed limit; wear a seat belt, drive in line with the weather conditions; never drink and drive, never drive if you're high, never text while driving, or get behind the wheel of a car if you're feeling tired.

4 Believe me, this is one of the less disturbing images. Safety Tip: Keep to the speed limits appropriate for the weather conditions.

But I was extremely grateful for the heads-up. In many ways, seeing those photographs at least readied me for the many years of emotional turbulence ahead, though the process was very one-dimensional. Nothing ever truly prepares you for the sensory overload that accompanies a motorway pile-up – the smell of death and the taste of burning petrol and rubber, the sound of suffering, holding a floodlight above a Helicopter Emergency Medical Service (HEMS) doctor while they perform open-heart surgery on an unconscious driver on the motorway. The experience is always smothering and traumatic.

Many years later, I received a first-hand insight into just how preoccupied Doctor Death had become with his work. I'd been waiting for treatment in the local A&E ward, having been injured while working at a road traffic collision. A car was burning on the side of the road and after extinguishing the blaze, I took off my breathing apparatus and inspected the vehicle. The bonnet had popped open, exposing the guts and vital organs of the vehicle when . . . BANG! The battery exploded, unable to contain the pressure that was building up inside – a result of the intense heat in the car. Battery acid scorched my face and eyes. I was in agony, barely able to see, and before too long, I was receiving treatment in a curtained cubicle at the local hospital when unexpectedly, a head popped through a gap in the drapes: it was Doctor Death and he was leering at me. He loved a hospital.

'Hey, Leigh,' he barked in a soft, Irish accent. 'For Christ's sake, what are you doing here at four in the morning?'

I could have asked him the same question. His floating head resembled that memorable scene from *The Shining* – Jack Nicholson's character Jack Torrance peers manically through a shredded hole in the bathroom door, having attacked it with an axe. Reluctantly, I told him the sorry tale.

'So, why are you here?' I asked.

'Well, Leigh, I care about all my firefighters, you know that,' he said. 'I'll give you a lift home once they've discharged you.'

His head retreated from the gap in the curtains, only to briefly reappear a few minutes later.

Retired now, Doctor Death was one of the best and one of the nicest officers I ever had the pleasure of working with and he shaped the careers of hundreds of fire officers.

Over the weeks and lots of graft, I got the hang of making hose up and decided to fight fire with fire, though not literally – that would have been pretty reckless of me. Instead, I decided that revenge is a dish best served cold, and one morning, as I neared the end of my training, I noticed the sub-officer, *my nemesis*, pulling up in the car park. I'd heard rumours that he tended to leave his car unlocked, having figured that no one would be stupid enough to mess with him. *Big mistake!* That morning, having watched him grunt at me as I cleaned a stack of equipment in the appliance bay, I decided the time to test that theory had arrived. I dropped to my hands and knees to avoid the attentions of any passing officers and commando-crawled towards his motor, reaching up to check the handle on the driver's side.

Fuck me, it was unlocked!

Right, I thought, smiling, *it's time. Yeah, I should know better, but bollocks to that. What goes around comes around.*

Guessing the sub-officer would probably stick around in his office for at least a few hours, I wriggled back to the appliance bay and finished off my work, then went to the locker room with a hole punch and a stack of A4 paper. For the best part of an hour, I stuffed a carrier bag with small, circular cuts, much to the amusement of my fellow recruits, who couldn't believe what I was about to attempt. Everybody knew I'd be for it if I got caught. *But I wasn't about to get caught.* Moments later, I was back in the appliance bay, where I grabbed a plastic funnel before crawling my way back towards the sub-officer's car. Once inside, I opened up the air conditioning vents in his dashboard and poured handfuls of the white paper discs inside, making sure to sweep out any evidence in the footwells as I left the scene. Then I flipped the vents open, knowing they were likely to explode at full blast when the engine and air con was turned on, before wriggling back to my day.

I didn't have to hang around for long before the fireworks exploded. As an eerie sense of paranoia began to creep over me, I watched the sub-officer walking back to his car. My adrenaline soared.

Here we go, I thought, *death or glory time.*

Having taken up position with the rest of the squad at an upper staircase window, I waited as my victim opened the door of his car and fumbled around for his ignition keys. Nineteen other recruit firefighters had gathered around me to share in the moment as I studied the fully-recyclable dirty bomb waiting to go off below. The engine spluttered. My heart pounded. As I heard the radio start, my adrenaline soared. Then, a split second later, the sub-officer's car seemed to transform into a kid's Christmas snow globe, the type you shake and admire, as tens of thousands of small paper discs billowed into the nooks and crannies of his interior.

'Bloody hell, Leigh!' I heard a laughing voice behind me say. 'You're in so much trouble, he'll be finding those things for months.'

Oh, shit! I'd gone too far, and any doubts regarding the kickback to my prank were wiped away instantaneously. The engine was turned off and it was just possible to hear a very angry man ranting and raving below in an expletive-peppered moment.

'BASTARDS!' yelled the sub-officer. 'Who's done this?'

He was out of his car now and covered in the paper discs too. Then he stared up at the first-floor windows of the training centre, jabbing a finger furiously.

'If the person that's done this isn't down here in five minutes to clear it all up, you're all in so much trouble on Monday morning!' he snapped.

I felt the watch staring at me again. 'Fessing up was the right thing to do, I knew that, but I also knew that there was a good chance I might lose my job before I'd even emerged from training.

'Listen, if I go down there, he's going to kill me,' I said. 'My career might go down the pan.'

The other recruits, understanding my predicament, accepted the decision. No one breathed a word, even when we were forced into a gruelling hour-long session of push-ups, burpees and squat thrusts the following Monday. The pain I could handle. As far as I was concerned, it had been worth it, just to see the look on my nemesis's face.

The culmination of the entire programme was the Breathing Apparatus (BA) training – a gruelling, three-week course where, for the most part, I crawled around on my hands and knees through chambers of extreme heat and thick smoke and the reason you'll never meet a firefighter with nyctophobia.[5] Thankfully, I was wearing all the protective gear required for such a task: fire gear, helmet, boots, gloves and breathing apparatus. This training was tough – physically, emotionally and mentally, but essential. I learned how to operate effectively in extremely hot and punishing conditions and was taught how to search for and find people inside these hostile environments with zero visibility, as well as being shown the best methods for extricating them to safety.

I learned how to master my air supply efficiently and safely in the harshest of environments and if the worst came to the worst and I found myself in trouble, I knew how to escape while sharing a colleague's air supply. Instructions were also given on the best ways to safely access and use stairs during an inferno, even while carrying a casualty.

I was also schooled in how to use a guideline – a 60m line that a team of firefighters would lay when penetrating a large smoke-filled building, tying it off at suitable

---

5 It means fear of the dark, for those of you who don't watch *The Chase*.

intervals and extending if necessary, so that following teams could then clip onto it when going deep into the structure. Essentially, it enabled a BA team to find their way in and out safely and quickly. But I was thankful for every scrap of that tuition and intelligence – it helped to keep me alive early on in my operational career.

It was obvious why so much info was being drilled into the recruits. Stepping into a burning building was the riskiest part of the job, no question. Many of the firefighters who have died in the line of duty have done so while wearing breathing apparatus. It was for that reason the training for this skill was the most intense part of the seventeen weeks. Wannabe firefighters without the minerals to function in those conditions were quickly told to think about another profession. And bloody hell, did they put us through the wringer!

The last assessment was no joke – the third week was spent at a specialist training facility where we worked through flashover and backdraft simulations. These events were intense and very hot. I had to manage compartment fires and search for casualties in temperatures of around 600°F, where the only way to get the job done was on your hands and knees, or lower. Wriggling through a room on my belly was considered a viable tactic. Backdraft and flashover simulations were just about the closest anybody could get to The Real Thing.

The final test required me and another squad member to save a heavy, but lifelike drill dummy from a burning simulation building. Fire rolled up the walls and flour-ished across the ceilings and I remember one thought as I prepared to unleash several gallons of water onto the flames: *Take it easy on the hose reel. You'll steam everyone like a boil-in-the-bag dinner.* But having dealt with the fire, compartment-by-compartment, searching and clearing rooms as we went, we soon found our mock casualty and exited to safety. We'd done it! Shortly afterwards, I was told I'd passed with flying colours.

I was going to make it as a firefighter.

The emotions on passing out were mixed. I was proud, no question; it felt great to know that I was going to extend my family's lineage into the Service. There was also a certain sense of relief. I'd silenced anyone who doubted whether I could match the standards set by Dad and Grandad – I *did* have what was required to be a firefighter. But there was trepidation, too. Passing the training course was really only the first in a series of steps when making the grade. I'd soon find myself working through a probationary period set to last four years, where I'd have to put all the skills I'd learned into practice, in troublesome situations where lives would be on the line. I'd be using my breathing apparatus in do-or-die events. Witnessing bloody injuries in the aftermath of a high-speed traffic collision would become a regular occurrence. I was about to be exposed to the heartbreak and horror that only a house fire can create. No photographs or re-construction video could truly ready me for the events to come, but at least I could hold my head high.

I'd only gone and bloody done it!

Every passing recruit was given a fortnight's holiday and on our return we prepared for a display drill attended by our friends and family in what is regarded by all firefighters as a pretty momentous event. The Chief Fire Officer of the Service stood up and explained what would be expected of us in the years to come. We might have qualified but there was to be no room for complacency. Over the next four years, we would have to study for exams and work through various training programmes but for the rest of my working life, my life and the lives of others depended on a zero-tolerance attitude towards failure. At least I had a new family to support me.

On the night of that passing-out parade, I got hammered. Our squad of probationary firefighters staggered from bar to bar and we ended up in a nightclub until the early hours of the morning. A minibus dropped us back at the training centre, where we all slept on the floor in the appliance bay, but not before we were able to exact a little revenge on our training officers for the thrashings of the past seventeen weeks. Somewhat sensibly, they had locked themselves in an office to sleep, aware that some of us might have scores to settle. But having scaled a ladder with a length of hose reel, we were able to prise open a window. The order came to turn on the taps and gallons of water doused the room, soaking the shouting occupants so they were wet through. As I ran back to my bed and pretended to be asleep, I could still hear them shouting and swearing – I was now officially part of the family.

5

When the Bells Go Down

I've watched a lot of documentaries about firefighters around the world. I think all firefighters probably do. More than any other, one sticks in my memory, though I can't for the life of me remember the name of it. A documentary crew had been trailing a watch from one particular firehouse in New York, which included a rookie firefighter. For weeks they'd waited around for something, *anything*, to happen, until finally, during an interview with the new recruit, he moaned about the distinct lack of action. The poor kid wasn't happy. For about a month he'd done nothing more than extinguish the odd dumpster fire. The newbie then stated a well-known fact about those early days on the job: 'The longer you wait for your first proper fire, the bigger it's bound be.' Having made this announcement, the date of the interview flashed upon the screen:

10 September 2001

It's a fundamental truth of the job: you wait around, desperate for something to happen, even though you know that something may be bad news.

I've watched massive incidents unfold on the news and understood the emotions that would have been churning through every individual working on the ground. When the Twin Towers of the World Trade Center came down on 11 September 2001, I was off duty, painting my porch when the call came through from a mate that something was kicking off in New York City. In those haunting hours that followed, I was glued to the telly, thinking, *Shit, those things are coming down* . . . I understood how fire compromises a structure. I also knew that reinforced concrete eventually gives way under extreme heat and how structural steelwork becomes soft when exposed to incredibly high temperatures. It only needed one chunk of tower to give way before the whole thing collapsed in on itself like a pyramid of playing cards. But then there was the professional viewpoint. I wondered: 'How many people are those firefighters going to save before it comes down?' And, 'How many firefighters are about to be killed?'

Despite the inevitable horrors, every man and woman preparing to hurry into that hell would have felt excited and adrenalised. I knew because that's how I too would have felt. There's always a buzz when I'm pulling on a breathing apparatus set, waiting to go into a burning building, knowing there might be a chance I could save someone else's life. Not a lot of people can get their head around that thought process and it's what separates the people squirting water onto a fire to pay the bills from those who earn a living by doing something much more sensible.

Thanks to my dad and grandad, I understood many of these truths, way before my first day in the job. I knew that the connection bonding every man and woman in the Fire Service would help to keep me alive, as much as my breathing apparatus and protective equipment. Most of all, I was told that humour was a glue: it would stick me to whatever watch I ended up with, and practical jokes were going to help me pass the time while I waited around for the next shout to come in. Wind-ups, funny war stories and mickey taking would all distract my thoughts from whatever tragedy the watch had recently endured. And the laughter that ran through every fire station in the country was the lifeblood of what could be, at times, a distressing and terrifying occupation. To not play the fool at times would be to think too much – and to think too much would invite all sorts of horrors into our lives.

During those early days in the Fire Service, I had to wait ages for my first big call. And for months and months all I seemed to do was practise and practise again, waiting for the opportunity to put my skills to use. The station I'd been sent to was known in the Service as 'The Second Worst Posting in the Brigade', owing to the fact that it only received around 450 shouts a year on average.[1] Those events were split over four watches and given that the majority of them were false alarms – because the public could sometimes be a little overdramatic – or minor incidents, the chances of my getting a decent fire seemed few and far between. Don't get me wrong, I wasn't wishing misfortune upon others. I didn't

---

1 On my first day on duty, one of the senior firefighters advised me not to bother looking out of the window in the morning. When I asked why, he responded, 'Because you'll have fuck all to do in the afternoon.'

want people to get hurt just so I could get a surge of adrenaline, or job satisfaction. Instead it was frustrating to know that I wasn't going to be able to put myself in harm's way to help others as frequently as I'd have liked. Friends and people who weren't in the job weren't able to comprehend my thought process but that's where I wanted to be, in the thick of it, like everyone else that had operated in the emergency services, past and present – like Grandad, my uncle and my dad.

I was becoming frustrated and very grumpy.

'I'm never gonna see a fire,' I moaned to my dad one night. 'I'm never gonna see a traffic collision . . . All that stuff I joined for just isn't going to happen.'

Dad nodded sagely and then smiled: 'You just wait,' he said.

I pulled cats from trees and helped to conduct a number of safety inspections. Then the local paper became very excited about a spate of bin fires, which were then blamed on some particularly anarchic youths in the area.[2] A humorous highlight eventually arrived when I had to cut a teenager from a kiddies' swing – the herbert had wedged himself in for shits and giggles (I'll tell you more about that one a little later). Other than that, I spent my time waiting for the first big event. And waiting. And then waiting even more until my FOMO was off the charts. It didn't help that I was reminded of all the tales of selfless endeavour from my dad and grandad; I kept hearing of events coming in at the busier stations in the area. And then during a relief shift at another station,

---

2 No one ever wants to be a firefighter as a kid to put out bin fires.

where I had to cover someone who had taken leave, a shout came in: it was a proper fire. *My first.* And boy, it was noteworthy!

The 999 details appeared on the station's watch room printer:

Fire in a large antiques warehouse.

Multiple calls received.

Extra resources mobilised due to business type and premises construction.

The lights had come up at the station. People moved at an urgent pace. Blue lights flashed and sirens wailed on our engines.

Bloody hell! I thought. *This is it, the big one!*

As in most careers, a firefighter never forgets the first time they're called into action for real. The first 999 call to that first barn burning inferno; their first run into a building on the verge of implosion to save the life of someone they've never met before, and might never see again. The first flash of mortal reality: *I might not get out of here alive.* And inevitably, the first unforgettable rush of adrenaline, a surge so exciting there's every chance they might piss their pants on the spot because they know that death or life-changing injury is a very real and painful possibility. Although it sounds terrifying, it's also the moment every firefighter passing their basic training dreams of. As we travelled to the warehouse at speed, the traffic parting in front of us, all of those emotions seemed to hit me at once.

This was the fire engine I'd seen as a kid flying by, but this time I was sitting on it.

But going into that first job seemed very surreal. I suppose I'd been anticipating it for so long that it was always going to feel weird. My emotions were all over the shop. I felt excited for sure, but also respectful, because living in and around the consequences of fire and hearing the stories that Dad had told me had readied me for handling a blaze, both practically and psychologically. I knew I wasn't frightened, but wary? Yeah. Respectful? *Oh, you better believe it!* But scared? *No way!* I didn't know fear, not during my upbringing, and not then. The only worries I had at that time in my life revolved around my family and the stress of something happening to someone I loved.

When it came to the challenges I was set to face during the antiques warehouse fire, all the normal anxieties experienced by normal people, such as the horror of being buried or burned alive, or of seeing a colleague die on the job, were replaced by a sharpening of the senses. I felt switched on. My body seemed to brim with adrenaline, which was a tool I knew I'd need to get the job done. Strength in the face of adversity gives you control. Control heightens awareness and stops the self-preservation part of a rational brain causing apprehension. This inevitably ends up with your conscience screaming: 'What the hell are you doing running into a burning building?' Not a helpful dynamic when lives need saving.[3]

As I was to discover, a firefighter goes through several phases of preparation during the drive towards a shout. The

---

3 Another reason why we're constantly drilling and spending time in hot smoke-filled rooms. By repetition, you normalise it and by normalising it, you own any fear that could otherwise cause you to freeze, even for a couple of seconds.

first is often scepticism. I had been told that members of the public would often overplay an incident. For example, reports of a 'life-or-death' house fire were often better described as a smaller event that could be extinguished in next to no time. Cats got stuck up trees all the time – that was not an emergency. But if more and more calls came in for one particular incident, then the mood shifted to an acceptance that this was going to be a serious fire. En route to the warehouse, I ran through those same thought processes, feeling slightly sceptical. I wasn't entirely sure the fire was as big as the eyewitness reports were claiming. But when another call came in, and then another, all of them reporting the same blaze, my mood changed. This was it! I readied my breathing apparatus set as a series of instructions were issued to the watch.

'Listen in! Leigh, it's likely we will be committing BA crews. Your job will be to enter the warehouse with Jay,' shouted the officer-in-charge over the blaring sirens. 'Clip onto him and stay close. *Very close!*'

I looked across at Jay and felt a sense of relief. A highly experienced firefighter, I knew he'd have my back if anything went wrong.

The officer-in-charge had a quick recce, then said, 'You two, you're to enter the building with a charged hose reel and thermal imaging camera. You are my eyes on the inside, figure out if anything can be saved, or whether we're going to end up with a new car park in town.'[4]

After checking my PPE, helmet, gloves and air cylinder contents, I tightened the Velcro fixings on my firegear

---

4 A firefighter's description of a total building loss.

and fire hood. I looked over Jay's equipment and clothing as we steadied ourselves for My First Big Fire.

This was the one!

Don't piss yourself, Leigh, I thought to myself. *Don't piss yourself . . .*

The antiques warehouse was all sorts of messed-up. It was three storeys high, with a timber framework and smoke seemed to churn the tiled roof. A builder's worker told us how the insides comprised endless corridors of valuable inventory. Smoke throbbed from the windows; glass panes smashed and cracked with the heat. Even from a distance, the temperature seemed intense. A strong wind was whipping the smoke into a choking typhoon.

Jay and I approached, and I placed my hand on the warehouse entrance, pausing for a split second. Through my mask and helmet I could hear the inferno. It seemed to be roaring and anticipation prickled my skin with sweat. We took one last air gauge reading and entered the building.

Jay nodded towards a door at the end of the first compartment. The fire was somewhere on the other side.

We needed to investigate.

Beyond this door the scene in the warehouse was as intimidating as anything I could have imagined. God knows what the original heat source had been during this particular Triangle of Fire, but the fuel was easy to identify. Vintage chairs, wardrobes and knick-knacks were burning, breaking apart in the heat. They had become brittle and dry from years and years of being in storage and I could tell the fire was also rapidly consuming all the air inside the warehouse. The flames around the building flickered slowly and their intensity was diminishing slightly, but a vacuum of negative pressure was building as the fire searched for more oxygen. This was bad news. If another window exploded, or a door opened, it might allow for a draft to be sucked in. The vacuum would be filled again with fresh air and there was a good chance that the reaction would create a super-heated gas explosion, igniting everything in its path at 700°C.

Nothing would survive.

In that last week of BA training we were taught that the best tactic in moments of this kind was to open the door slowly, have a listen, pump a quick pulse of water into the ceiling area of the room and wait to see if it instantly vaporised. I turned the handle, my foot wedged against the wood to stop any pressure or flames from blowing the door outwards. Jay pulsed the hose-reel branch for a second, maybe two – no bangs, no hissing. Result! We quickly stepped in. The water also hadn't turned to steam, which was a good sign that the conditions inside wouldn't be too punishing. Inside, shelves and shelves of inventory were burning. Smoke was gathering in the rafters of the warehouse and slowly falling, filling the room, creating a neutral plane – a hellish environment in which dark, swirling fogs tended to build at the top of the room. If I were to reach up, putting my hand into the plane, it would disappear, leaving a straight line of clear air at the wrist. The more smoke produced, the further the neutral plane would fall, increasing the air pressure below it. I'd been taught to expect my ears to pop – it's an interesting environment to work in.

Jay and I knew we had a little bit of time. The neutral plane was still fairly high, the smoke still grey in colour. That meant the building wouldn't have been at the point of collapse just yet. We also knew there wasn't anyone reported missing in the warehouse, so our only task was to check if anything could be saved, including the timber building itself. This was a very dynamic assessment that we could make by reading the signs around us and respecting what we could see, while relying heavily on experience (in Jay's case) and gut feeling (mine). By the looks of it, there was plenty of furniture that could be salvaged and the building too. If we were able to put the fire out in time, that is.

A moment later, Jay tapped me on the shoulder. He was pointing upwards and I could see a flicker of urgency in his eyes: the smoke was changing. I watched it morph from light to dark and then into something more psychedelic. Tentacles of yellow and mustard curled outwards and they were thickening. The neutral plane was lowering. *The inferno was hungry again.* Running low on oxygen, it had begun its search for more. If it reached a source, such as a broken window or a gap in the door behind us, all that pent-up energy would explode, taking me, Jay and the warehouse with it. Then my ears popped . . .

The conditions were rapidly deteriorating, the signs were bad.

We'd outstayed our welcome.

'Let's go!' shouted Jay. 'Run!'

Within seconds, the fire had engulfed the interior of the warehouse. Heat, fuel and oxygen had all come together violently and flames were soon crawling across the ceiling and down the walls. We wasted no time and exited through the door we came in. *WHOOSH!* A scorching backdraft closely followed. Had we waited a moment longer, further crews would have been required to save our arses because there was no way we would have got out on our own. As we stood outside, panting and buzzing, still in one piece, I breathed a sigh of relief. Hindsight's always 20:20, but I knew that salvaging any property from that building would have been impossible, even for the most experienced members on the watch. And for that, I felt a little sore, but at least we were still alive.

I heard our officer-in-charge's voice in my earpiece: 'You two OK?'

Jay looked at me and nodded. 'Yes, guv,' he said.

Finally, I'd experienced my first real fire.

Over the course of my career, the muscle memory reflexes and procedures associated with a proper shout eventually came to feel familiar and repetitive. But in those early years, every call arrived with a charge of excitement. The process had long been given a description – 'when the bells go down' – and this was borne from the fact that during its previous iterations, a bell had clanged throughout the fire station in order to alert the watch to a shout. Like coiled springs, everybody sprang into action and not a lot has changed these days. Certainly, the technology required for firefighting has been updated. All our equipment carries a modern upgrade on an historically familiar design, particularly the uniforms, plus the engine's sirens and flashing lights are not only effective, they're traditional. The way in which we organise ourselves now is significantly safer, too. But the emotions, not to mention the camaraderie, humour and bravery of every firefighter in the job, are still very much the same.

But what actually happens in a station when the bells go down?

Well, let's use a standard house fire scenario. There's a fire in the house.[5] You've got your kids out of their beds, Harry and Meghan the corgis are with you too, but there's nowhere to run. The flames are raging downstairs, they're out of control, and in the smoke and heat you've become disorientated, confused. That ear-splitting fire alarm isn't helping matters, either. Luckily, you've been forewarned. Leading everyone into the bedroom nearest the main street, you shut the door behind you, pushing a mattress against the frame to reduce the amount of smoke that might enter the space; you open a window and then call 999. The operator calmly connects you to the Fire Service.

'Fire & Rescue Service. What's the address of the emergency?'

You give your address to the Fire Control Operator, adding that you and your family have taken refuge in the bedroom nearest the street.

'Please hurry!'

The Operator then says, 'Stay calm, keep everyone together at the window, we're on our way. Stay where you are. Don't leave that room!'

The Fire Control swoops into action. Within seconds three fire appliances will be mobilised to you. If you're

---

5 You know this because you installed a smoke alarm. And regularly checked its batteries. See, I told you I was going to keep on about it!

lucky enough to have a local fire station near your home, firefighters can be with you in no time at all. But what happens during that time is so important because it can mean, quite literally, the difference between life and death. Brigades have dedicated Fire Control centres and it's these incredible hubs, with their amazing staff, that decide which fire stations attend which incidents, as well as the number of appliances required for the incident type. This is assisted by the geographical positioning systems found on all modern fire appliances, alongside sophisticated congestion algorithm software. It's been decided that three engines will be sent to your house.

Your 999 call is a time-critical event. Your local fire station instantly becomes a hive of activity. The mobilising alert lighting comes on, followed shortly afterwards by the bells going down. In a burst of momentum, men and women run to their appliances. The driver unplugs the vehicle-charging lead as firefighters pull on their PPE before mounting the engine. Yes, fire leggings are still, classically, unrolled upwards from over-the-fire boots. And as everybody readies their kit, the station's officer-in-charge tears off the tip sheet sent from Fire Control.[6] All the available information for your shout is on here – that way he, or she, can start to formulate a tactical plan.

But there's no time to stop and plan as a group. The officer-in-charge jumps onto the engine, and in

---

6 'Tip sheet' is our name for the incident printouts sent through to the station by Fire Control. The expression refers to us being tipped out of our bunks at night. We don't actually get tipped out of our bunks though, it's just an expression.

conjunction with the driver and crew, they figure out the quickest route to the incident and proceed.

Nowadays, the concept of health and safety is key to our wellbeing, and unlike the Fire Service of my dad and grandad's era, seat belts are a must because driving at high speed through an urban area brings its own set of risks. The watch then readies what it can from the strapped-in confines of the cab. Thermal imaging cameras, breathing apparatus sets and helmets are readied, though it's considered unsafe to put them on until the engine has come to a stop at the incident scene. Nevertheless, it definitely helps to be as ready as possible, so most firefighters will have spent their time on the road checking their PPE, while looking over their mate's straps and kit too.

En route, the officer-in-charge verbalises any additional information that might have been sent to the appliance from Fire Control regarding your incident. He or she says, 'Everybody listen in. We're going to a house fire; persons reported, 24 Avenue Road. Control say they're receiving a significant number of calls to this incident and have mobilised an additional appliance, they've requested an ambulance too. Significantly, the first call was from the family trapped inside.'

Tasks are delegated. Most modern-day fire engines are equipped with computer tablets, so it's sometimes possible to receive updates on any situation in real-time. On other occasions, a crew will be told over the main digital airwave radio that an incident they were speeding towards was actually a false alarm and they should stand down. But overall, firefighters will treat every job with respect. Believe me, the driver won't take their feet off the pedal until it's been officially announced that the Fire Service's assistance is no longer required. Likewise, if events have taken a turn for the worse – for example, if you're on the phone to Fire Control to tell us that the fire has reached the door of the room you've taken shelter in – the officer-in-charge will make a very considered and calculated decision based on a pros and cons assessment, risk versus gain. On those occasions, it may be necessary for the crew to operate outside of normal working practices. Firefighters in this situation will get rigged into their breathing apparatus en route in order to hit the ground running on arrival. Those individuals will be 'under air' and ready to go immediately. On more than one occasion I have witnessed those saved seconds proving instrumental to saving people trapped in burning buildings. Luckily, you are not in this position.

Instructions are arriving at speed now. The engine is pulling into Avenue Road. 'They're obviously *very* smart,' continues the officer-in-charge, 'because they've barricaded themselves into a bedroom nearest the street, shoved a mattress against the door to block the smoke and gathered at the window. Our first job is to get them out. Priority number one: get a ladder up to that window.'

The officer-in-charge is now pointing to where you are standing, waving and shouting. You can see them through the billowing smoke.

How a firefighter mentally prepares while stepping into an incident depends on the individual. It's now been twenty-five years since I graduated, but I'll still run through the same thought processes as I did when I was a new recruit. I remind myself of the dos and don'ts of a fire; I consider the safety and wellbeing of my watch, as well as myself. At times, I remember specific lessons from those early days as a probationary firefighter, particularly if they were focused on any procedures that might be required for the latest job. There's a lot of stuff going on in a firefighter's head when they get a shout, so a lot of us compartmentalise what we have to do in order to function effectively. There's no point worrying about what everyone else is doing. Instead it's far more beneficial to focus on your own role, trusting that everyone else will do theirs, synchronising as a team. The pump operator will be thinking about water supplies and water delivery. The BA crews will be concentrating on where they have to go in order to access the house and extinguish the fire. The officer-in-charge will manage the entire operation, smoothly and safely. All those moving parts add up to a phenomenally effective team.

The ladder goes up. You and your family are assisted down. Harry and Meghan the corgis are rescued.

There can be tears and anger, there might even be a distressing flashpoint, but overall, everybody has emerged in relatively good shape. All because the procedures for dealing with house fires have for decades undergone regular episodes of trial and error. And all because you followed the simple safety measures required to survive.[7]

I've put out hundreds of fires now, sat on my way to hundreds more jobs, but that first one is still burned into my memory.

---

7 Safety tip: Make sure you and your family have an emergency plan in place for what you would all do if a fire occurs in your house in the early hours. Rehearse it and keep it up to date. That plus a working smoke alarm on every floor of your house is the best preparation you can make.

6

A Brief Interlude on
What to Do if a Fire Starts

Having just taken you into a fire, it's only natural you'll be thinking about what you'd do if one happened in your own home. This healthy level of paranoia is a good thing. If everybody reading this was to make just one or two changes to their routines at home, it might help to reduce my workload, plus that of my colleagues the country over. At the very least it could prevent anybody from having to suffer the awkwardness of watching a Fire Investigation team rummage through a private storage space usually reserved for underwear and sex toys.

First of all, let's imagine the worst-case scenario: *A fire has started in the family home.* And you know this is because you *didn't* take the batteries out of the smoke alarm the last time it was triggered by a burning round of toast. There are two kids in the house, plus your partner and a cat and a dog. What do you do first? *Do you call the Fire Brigade, grab the kids, the pets and try to get to a window? Or do you grab the kids, forget the pets and try to escape, calling 999 once the family is safely outside?* Tricky, isn't it? Chances are you'll be in a state of panic too, so thinking on your feet won't come easily, especially if the building is filling up with thick, acrid, choking smoke. In those conditions it's impossible to see beyond the nose. The temperatures in the building will rise to unbearable levels too. Luckily, with a little forward thinking, all of these horrific questions can be answered in advance.

The first thing to do is to plan an escape route in the event of a house fire. Step one is to designate someone to grab the kids. The second is to build a clear idea of how to get everybody out of the building safely. You'd be horrified to learn just how many people haven't made it out of their homes in time because the keys to their front or back door were stashed deep in a desk drawer, or a plant pot. Keeping them out of clear sight and touch might feel like the most sensible idea when assessing the security of your property. However, if you're crawling around on your hands and knees in the pitch-black, you'll wish they were somewhere a little more accessible. My tip would be to keep the keys in the same spot, preferably in the door or somewhere easily reached, where you can locate them in a blind panic.

OK, before I impart my next bit of advice, I'd like to stress the fact that I'm an animal lover. I've happily saved cats, dogs, rabbits, snakes and guinea pigs from all sorts of places. But it's my job, not yours, so if Harry and Meghan, the family corgis, are stuck inside, please leave them for a trained specialist to rescue. If you can call the dog or cat and it comes to you, then great. If you can't, don't go back into the building to save it. If that sounds ruthless, I'm sorry, but one step into the thick of a house blaze will finish you off quite quickly. It only takes around two deep inhalations of smoke for a person to drop to the floor. After that, a stricken individual goes into respiratory arrest quite quickly. Oh, two quick tips: there's always cleaner oxygen to be found lower to the ground in a blaze, so crawl away if you're unable to run. And shut all the doors on the way out because it will slow the spreading flames, as well as reducing smoke damage throughout the house. (Just that one act, plus building and contents insurance, means that a damaged house can be made fairly habitable quite quickly in the fallout after a disaster.)

There is, of course, another nightmare scenario: the one in which you *can't* escape the house. If that's the case, all get into the room nearest to the street, because that's where we'll be showing up, blue lights blazing. Barricade the door with a mattress to reduce the amount of smoke entering the room. Open all the windows and call 999, making sure to explain your position: *My house is on fire! We're stuck inside 24 Avenue Road, but I'm in the first-floor bedroom on the side street where you'll be arriving.* Every fire appliance en route to the incident will have the information relayed to them so they can prepare in transit. Having received that intel, their first priority will be to get a ladder to your window in order to rescue everyone trapped inside. Of course, if you can get out of that window and onto a ledge or flat roof without injuring yourself, do so. Then shout. It might be there's a window-cleaning neighbour nearby who can lean their ladder into your position.

Now let's get down to the brass tacks. If you really want to fireproof your life, run through a mock fire drill with the family in advance. Turn off the lights and blindfold yourselves, because – believe me – the power in most buildings tends to go off pretty quickly in the event of a blaze (always take a fully charged mobile with you wherever you go because landlines also tend to get knocked out quite quickly in the event of a power failure). And with all the smoke associated with a house fire, you won't be able to see a thing. Practise evacuating the building on your hands and knees, making sure to exit by first finding the keys to whichever door you'll be using. (It'll also be noisy, what with the smoke alarms going off and the roar of the flames, so maybe ask Alexa to play some Slipknot at full blast.) If that sounds crazy, that's because it is, but nothing's quite as manic as finding an escape route in a burning building. The good news is that people like me will be on hand to help not too long after the first 999 call has been made. But until then you're on your own so give yourself a fighting chance of survival.

And buy those bloody smoke alarms!

7

The Longest Road

When I had complained to my dad that I hadn't seen any action, it was for two main rites of passage – a big blaze and a traffic collision. With one down, there was still one to go. But if you'd asked me now, I'd tell you I wish I'd never seen my first one.

If you treated it like a *Family Fortunes* question and asked a hundred people what firefighters responded to the most, then fighting fires would understandably score pretty highly.[1] But one aspect of the job that people still don't often think about is our role as first responders to road traffic collisions. On the way there's that sense of physical preparation as you're about to enter into a life-and-death scenario. With traffic collisions, though, we can't stop the car from crashing, we can't rewind time and untangle metal. We know that 'the golden hour' starts counting from the moment of impact to the time you enter the hospital. If we can get you there in that time, we know we've given you the best chance of survival. We all spend so much of our time

---

1 Along with rescuing cats from trees.

travelling at speed in our two-tonne metal boxes that we forget the damage they can do when things go wrong. Once you've seen your first traffic accident, you'll never forget, though.[2]

My first fatal car crash, in 2001, was something that affected me for quite some time afterwards, mainly because it was so gruesome – I honestly don't think I'll ever forget it. The memory is burned into my soul and in many ways it was further evidence that, despite Doctor Death's grisly picture collection, nothing could quite prepare a person for the visuals of a serious road traffic collision. It's an assault on the senses, twisted metal and people. Funnily enough, any curiosity a person might have had about what death looks like quickly disappears when reality bites for the first time. This individual had fallen asleep at the wheel of their car and crashed under the back of an HGV that was parked in a dual carriageway lay-by. The impact happened at high speed. The trailer was laden with large reinforced concrete construction slabs and there were no skid marks. The deceased's head was torn clean off, though there was some consolation in the realisation that they probably hadn't known a thing about it. My job at the scene was to help unpick the wreckage around the body so we could remove them. The work left a harrowing mark, one that would eventually affect me years down the line.

---

2 Safety tip: Always wear a seat belt and make sure your seat is far enough back from the airbag. Anything less than arm's length runs a risk of you being injured by the very thing that's supposed to protect you, as it deploys with explosive force. And if you ever turn your passenger airbag off, always remember to switch it back on.

Over the years, I've been to hundreds of car crashes. Physically, it's often difficult. A firefighter designated with the job of casualty care will have to twist and squeeze their way into the mangled metal. Once inside, the pressure is high too. It might be that the attending firefighter's first job is to manage an injured person's airway and C-spine – if they have a suspected back or neck issue – or stem any catastrophic bleeding from deep wounds until a paramedic arrives on the scene. One lapse of concentration can result in a tragic loss of life. There's also the element of fear. Car batteries overheat, exploding molten acid everywhere. If a fuel tank ruptures, it only needs one spark to set everything alight. In those situations, a firefighter would have to escape quickly in order to avoid being horrifically burnt. They'd then find themselves scarred with the guilt of leaving an injured person still pinned inside.

Whenever a driver or passenger is trapped in a car, someone like me will squeeze in alongside them until they've been freed. That process can sometimes take hours and the experience is often an ordeal for everyone involved. Hydraulic cutting tools and spreaders chew into the steel frame. The noise is always piercing; anyone nearby will feel as if their eardrums have ruptured. During those moments I'll hold the victim's hand and talk them through whatever's going on around them, so they can understand what the noises and vibrations are. I'll provide words of encouragement and optimism. Sometimes that can be the difference between a seriously injured person fighting to survive, or giving up and dying. But it can be hard to create a sense of hope sometimes, especially if someone's loved one has already died and is slumped next to them. None of the effort required in such a hectic situation comes easily.

For weeks and weeks after Road Traffic Collision training I had wondered what it might be like to see a cadaver for real. I almost wished it to happen, just so I could get it over and done with. The answer, when it came, was surreal and stomach churning.

The old-school approach to detailing road traffic collisions would almost certainly not happen now. A mindful safety bubble of risk mitigation is thrown up around firefighters these days, especially new recruits. While no one can be protected from all of the trauma of the work we do, it certainly helps to be entered into it in a slow and considered way. The feeling is that the chances of sensory overload are reduced by gradually introducing someone to serious emotional discomfort rather than dropping them in at the deep end. But I don't think that's the case, not really. Everybody's OK until they're not. All of us have different levels of tolerance to trauma. I thought I was fine for long periods of time after that first car wreck.

It don't bother me, I told myself.

I said the same thing to mates: 'I'm OK, honestly.'

My first road traffic collision incident was extreme. Most of the time, a firefighter will disconnect from death quite easily because they're not linked to the deceased. They might feel detached. It's possible to view the corpse from a distance. They seem real, but there's no soul and so the physical body seems artificial. It's as if their body is no more than a shell.[3] The biggest problem with a firefighter's role is that, generally speaking, no one dies peacefully in a house blaze or car crash. A paramedic, for example, will encounter a deceased who has passed away in their sleep peacefully, at home, in bed. But the most chilling reality for any firefighter is that every death they'll ever encounter will have come about in particularly unpleasant circumstances. And for some reason, it's often traffic collisions that really get to you.

My dad once told me a story he'd heard about a road traffic collision. The story goes that a bloke had been arguing with his girlfriend in the pub. She left, but having decided the arguing wasn't done, he then got in his car, pissed, and drove after her. At high speed on a blind bend, his vehicle slammed into an oncoming car. Somehow, he managed to survive with just a busted arm. The passengers in the other vehicle weren't so lucky – a mother and her son were killed.

When the Service arrived, the bloke was still ranting and raving; he was very combative, and wanted to get to his girlfriend. He had no idea he'd killed a mum and her kid. For some reason, this one really broke through and Dad was so upset and angry. *How do you recover from an experience like that?* His emotions were only heightened further when he heard the drunk driver received a lenient four-year sentence for his crime – causing death by dangerous driving. He was then released after two

---

3 As far as I'm concerned, that only adds to the sense that our bodies act like a vessel and there's a massive greater meaning to life than just being alive in this moment.

and a half years and the attending watch was in a fury afterwards. You can hardly blame them – they'd witnessed a horrific loss of life, but as we do they rallied around each other, accepted the sadness of the incident, and what their jobs entailed, and became closer and stronger for the experience. There was some sense of retribution in that the driver would be haunted for the remainder of his years, weighed down by the heaviest of burdens on his shoulders, but really, that was no consolation at all.

One particular accident that's always stayed with me happened some years ago. So tragic were the circumstances that in the days that followed I couldn't talk to anyone about it without my voice breaking.

We were called out to a collision between multiple cars and a lorry on a busy dual carriageway. It was one of those big supermarket delivery lorries and in a very unfortunate twist of fate a small family car had become entangled underneath it. There were two passengers who needed cutting free. I was first into the wreckage of this vehicle to assess the condition of the occupants while my colleagues stabilised and did what they could to make the vehicle safe. Extrication plans were made and we awaited the arrival of paramedics to triage the couple.

With me was a husband and wife, who must have been in their late sixties. The car had buckled down around them, keeping them pinned down in their seats and unable to see each other, but he was holding her hand tightly. The man was still conscious but his wife wasn't. My colleagues got to work. Paramedics had arrived and prioritised the release of the woman first. It's at this point of an extrication that it's vitally important to maintain dialogue with any conscious casualties. The noise that is generated from mechanical and hydraulic rescue tools can be very scary and overwhelming for some. Fortunately, this gentleman was suffering from so much shock that he wasn't really present in the moment. His thoughts were occupied by his wife's welfare. With a soft voice in among the intimidating bangs and vibrations, I did what I could. He told me they were travelling back from their home in the South of France to celebrate the forthcoming birth of their first grandchild. A planned C-section was to take place two days later. They'd been on the road fifteen hours and were only twenty-five minutes from their son's home.

'Is she alive, my wife, is she alive?'

'I'll check, hang on.'

I could see her chest rising and falling but her breaths were shallow and her pulse probably weak. I could also see that part of the metal of the car was pressed into her chest and abdomen. There was no way we were going to get her out of the seat without cutting away a chunk of the car. Even then, it was going to be painstaking work in constant consultation with the paramedics. Often in this sort of scenario, the metal of the car is all that's holding someone together and when you cut it away, their condition can rapidly deteriorate. It's a terrible burden to know that your actions might cause that but it's essential that we free them as quickly as possible.

'Yes, she's still alive.'

'Thank God,' he replied.

He didn't seem to have any injuries. There was nothing

that I was overly worried about, he was just wedged in firmly.

'So bloody close, we were so bloody close,' he kept murmuring. He reached out his other hand to me. 'Just tell me she's going to be all right, my Joan.'

Tragically, I couldn't see her chest moving anymore. I reached over and felt for a pulse in her neck, but couldn't find one. My colleagues were still creating space to get her out, but there was nothing I could do for her where she was, CPR (cardiopulmonary resuscitation) was an impossibility.

Paramedics declared her death a short time later and I in turn relayed this to her unsuspecting and devastated husband. A sheet was pulled across her and the crews then concentrated on releasing him. As I am sure you can imagine, this was an emotionally raw event. It was impossible to shut away my feelings and close my consciousness. I felt and absorbed so much of his pain.

I thought about all the things that had to happen for them to meet each other. For the exact combinations of all those generations of ancestors who had to meet to make them who they were, for them to fall in love and have a family, for their child to meet someone and fall in love, to have a child of their own. All the millions of choices and accidents. For them to turn the wrong way when the lorry was coming. For all of it to come down to that moment of me holding both their hands in a pile of twisted metal. I couldn't stop thinking about the look in his eye, desperate to know but also not to know.

When I arrived home the following morning and sat motionless at the kitchen table, when my wife gave me a hug and put me to bed, those were the thoughts that wouldn't leave my mind.

8

The Recruit

A few years back, a small blaze scorched a house on an estate on our fire ground. Luckily, very little had been damaged inside. Once the scene was cool, safe and ventilated, it was my job as the officer-in-charge to investigate the cause and by the looks of it, all evidence pointed to the bedroom. This tallied up with the neighbour's testimony, seeing smoke seeping from an upstairs window. But having nosed around, the ignition source was hard to establish. Other than a drawer full of burnt underwear, there was nothing.

Suddenly I heard a cough behind me: it was the home owner. She was looking at me with wide eyes. Instructing my colleague, Dave, to take over the search, I went over to explain the situation.

'Hi, don't worry, shocking though this is, it's not as bad as it looks,' I said, understanding the trauma that can shake a person when their neighbour has rung, telling them their house is on fire. 'By the looks of it, you've suffered more smoke damage than anything else . . .'

The woman kept looking past me at Dave as he inspected her dresser.

Was she in shock? I wondered.

'So anyway, check your insur—'

Suddenly Dave nudged me hard in the back. 'Right, that's us done,' he said, nodding politely at the home-owner as he brushed past. 'Turns out this was completely accidental. Sorry for the mess madam. Come on, guv . . .'

I followed him out, confused. 'Mate, what was that all about?'

But Dave looked awkward. 'Let's just say I found the, um, toy box.'

The toy box?

'Toys that adults play with.'

Now the penny dropped.

'I pulled the drawer out slightly to check at the back, that's when I saw and checked the charred box.'

'Was it electric? Do you think that's what started the fire?'

Dave shook his head. 'No, but there was a large crystal ornament on the windowsill. My guess is that the sun had hit it for a while, which had created a beam of light, like a magnifying glass onto her open underwear drawer. You know when kids kill ants with a magnifying glass? Yeah . . . *that.* The heat had caused something to smoulder and everything went up from there. The toys were in a box in the same drawer.'

No wonder the woman looked so keen for me to stop talking.

'Had it all melted?'

'No,' said Dave. 'Most of it was metal.'

Just about the only thing guaranteed for a recruit firefighter back then, in those first weeks and months on station is an episodic soap opera of comedy. From the minute their shiny new badge and uniform has been despatched, they'll often spend the first few days, weeks, sometimes months of their career suffering the slings and arrows associated with naivety and inexperience, each one fired by their new watch mates. That might sound harsh, but it's something everybody has to expect when arriving on a station. *Why?* Well, first, it's become a longstanding vocational tradition and a rite of passage for any cherubic-faced firefighter. Second, because it's a light-hearted exercise and tends to bring any new faces into the fire station family fairly quickly.

I'd grown up hearing about how important humour was as a way of dealing with the darkness of the job, but it was only now that I'd been to my first fire and seen my first fatality that I truly understood how important a bloody good laugh can be. As most firefighters will attest, there can sometimes be long periods of time between 999 calls, especially where I'd been assigned, where my first big fire hadn't heralded a sudden rush of action, and so bantering the wet-behind-the-ears a little bit is widely considered an entertaining pastime. Now, I know that every part of society is coming to terms with the fact that what once seemed like 'a bit of fun' from some angles, very much wasn't for some people and I've heard stories of things going too far. Luckily, I've never experienced it.

Having arrived on the scene with the reputations of both my dad and grandad looming over me, I very much got it in the neck. I was wound up, teased and spoofed. This process was intensified because a number of squad members had assumed my progression through the job would be assured owing to nepotism. One or two people wondered out loud whether I'd receive the same emotional roughhousing experienced by most probationary firefighters, but I knew there would be very little mercy. I'd certainly had enough of a warning of what to expect and Dad had told me about how his watch had pranked a new recruit on his first day during a training drill. The whole crew was set to work on an exercise using a foam-producing cannon on a fuel-fire scenario in the drill yard. Unbeknown to the newly landed recruit, everybody had applied red paint to their hands a day or so previously. After one or two washes it had faded enough for it to resemble an ugly rash.

'We're refusing to do the drill,' said one of the watch to the recruit. 'Look at our hands, they're fucked! It's the foam concentrate, there's something lethal in it. So, when the station commander comes out and details this foam drill, we're going to tell him to stick it. We're all in agreement on this one. Are you in, too?'

Not wishing to look like a lone wolf, the probationary firefighter nodded, enthusiastically: 'Yeah, I can do that.'

Shortly afterwards, the entire watch was on the training ground; the station commander was running through the preliminary details of the drill.

'Right, today, gentlemen, we're going to be carrying out a foam exercise, carrying on from last week,' he said. 'And we just want to get the application right. So, this will be the drill: we're going to get two lines of hose to work from the water tender and we're going to apply a blanket of foam to the floor at the base of the tower. Is everyone OK and happy to do the drill?'

The station commander turned to the rookie, who

was first in line for acknowledgement.

'No, sir, I'm not doing it,' he said, shaking his head.

The station commander looked taken aback. 'Hmm, OK,' he said. 'Not the best start to your career.' He then moved on to the next member of the watch. 'And what about you?'

'Yes, sir,' said the firefighter enthusiastically.

He moved on again. The next firefighter was also in agreement, as was the next one. *And the next* . . . The newbie had been left hanging out to dry.

The station commander returned to him with a stern look on his face.

'Right, take your fire gear off,' he said. 'I'll see you in my office, please.'

The poor recruit was crestfallen. He must have been wondering why his new colleagues had dropped him in it. *Had he offended someone?* Possibly, his fledgling career was flashing before his eyes. He was then left to stew on his decision for what felt like hours until eventually the station commander returned with a grin on his face.

'Right, all's forgiven,' he said. 'It was a wind-up and a lesson. All you need to remember throughout your career is this: all firefighters are wind-up merchants. You can join your watch now.'

The pranks during my first few months in the job seemed to be never-ending and I was very much on the receiving end of all of them. Thanks to those dinnertime stories I'd heard as a kid, I was fairly familiar with the type of jokes despatched by firefighters. That helped in heading off a few potentially chastening ambushes, but rather than dissuade my new teammates from dropping me in it, my situational awareness only inspired them to become even more creative. Their cause was helped by the fact that my family hadn't been tuned into every pitfall in the game. For example, when my dad had joined as a recruit, there hadn't even been a dishwasher in the station. If there had, he might have forewarned me of its role in a very modern ruse.

Every firefighter knows the importance of keeping the fire engines in pristine condition. No one wants to discover that a pump has failed in the middle of a job, or that the indicator light has broken while the watch surges through rush-hour traffic towards a five-car pile-up. The pumps in our station were checked and double-checked regularly, as they were in every station around the country, and whenever something packed up, it was often up to the freshest face in the station to call Control to request our Service workshops to come and take a look at the problem. Within a couple of hours, a fleet mechanic would have been despatched to fix whatever was on the blink.

As I've mentioned earlier, a fire engine can often be referred to as an 'appliance', and, as I was about to discover to my cost, it was a word that could be left open to interpretation in many ways. One night, as the watch settled down for dinner, a small drama kicked off. One of the lads was tinkering around with the dishwasher in the kitchen, muttering and swearing under his breath. Everybody was enjoying his building frustration, until, eventually, he began jabbing at the buttons in a rage.

'Oh, for fuck's sake!' he snapped, finally. 'The dishwasher's packed up again. We're going to have to wash up by hand tonight.'

There was a collective groan. Then the officer-in-charge said, 'There's a job for you, Leigh.'

'What do you mean, guv?' I said.

'Well, get on to Control and tell them that one of our appliances has packed up.'

'Hang on,' I said, confused. 'I get that this is a *kitchen* appliance, but I thought Control only dealt with the engine appliances? I know where this is going: I'm going to ring Control and I'm going to look like a right mug, aren't I? Then they're going to say, "Your dad's been in the job long enough. Shouldn't you know better?"'

The mess wasn't having it, though.

'Just do it, Leigh. You'll see . . .'

It was time to suck up any reservations I was experiencing about what might or might not have been a wind-up. I reached for the phone that linked our station with Control and made the call, waiting for the inevitable sniggering at the other end.

As previously explained, Fire Control notifies us where to go and what type of incident we're going to, keeping us safe during incidents by relaying intelligence that isn't immediately available to us on the ground, such as wind direction or possible toxic materials that might be reported to be burning away in a warehouse fire. But they were also on hand to deal with any small-scale issues we might be having at the station, particularly if it involved any important, life-saving equipment. As the phone rang, I worried how my request might seem like a massive waste of their time.

'Yeah, so we've got a faulty appliance,' I said warily when the call was eventually answered. It was hard not to feel a little exposed. 'I want to book one "off the run".'[1]

'Oh, OK,' said Control. 'Which appliance is it?'

'The Zanussi dishwasher, it's in our mess.'

There was a pause and some muffled laughter.

Here we go, I thought.

'Sure, no problem,' replied the voice. 'Can you get the serial number for it, please?'

'Er, yeah,' I replied, feeling a little confused and walked back to the mess where the watch were eating and watching the football on the telly. Ignoring the laughter and snarky comments, I was soon on my hands and knees, manoeuvring the bulky dishwasher out of its storage space and peering around the back with a torch. Having scribbled down the relevant digits, I was able to book a mechanic, satisfied I hadn't been on the wrong end of yet another humiliating wind-up.

This drama went on for months, though – the dishwasher was an old wreck and tended to pack up every few weeks, at which point I was always ordered to book another appliance defect. The responsibility was only passed down after I'd spent six months at the station and

---

1 'Off the run' or 'on the run' is an old Victorian firefighting term. In those days, the fire steam carts pulled by horses were very heavy. At stations the cartwheels were hauled onto a slightly inclined ramp when they weren't being used (called a 'run'). To hold them in place the carts were 'chocked' with wooden wheel blocks. When a fire was reported the chocks were pulled out, allowing the cart to start rolling, which made it far easier for the horses to start pulling the momentum. When a cart was available it was described as being 'on the run'. Unavailable, it was referred to as being 'off the run'. These terms are still used today.

another probationary firefighter joined the watch. The relief at not having to call in to Control in order to beg for another dishwasher maintenance number felt huge, but there was a sting in the tail during the handover period.

'Leigh, can you go and ring Control up,' whispered a colleague from the watch one morning. 'Tell them we've got a new recruit and we're going carry on with the appliance prank.'

Despite my confidence, I'd been getting screwed over all along. But, boy, did I enjoy being on the other side of the joke when my moment came along.

I'd got off fairly lightly, though. Some of the tales regarding the pranks pulled on firefighting newbies are now etched into legend and no new addition to a watch was spared their introductory trial by fire. Though I'd like to point out, *not literally*. We were very professional when it came to the devastating combination of heat, fuel and air within confined spaces and other emergenices. Instead, the jokes were played out during those down-times in the station when we weren't performing drills or fire safety inspections. If a community was having a particularly good run of luck, days, or even weeks could pass between house fires and stranded cat events. Within those periods of time, when the brain was left with very little to focus upon, it became hard not to dream up a new and imaginative stitch-up for the new face.

We were hardly unique, though. Any number of building site apprentices will tell you about the time they were messed around on day one of their new career because their site manager had sent them off to a hardware store in order to pick up a mythical piece of equipment.

The new recruit swallowed any reservations they might have had about ordering a tin of tartan paint, or a spirit level bubble from the local Homebase and pressed ahead regardless, despite being 99 per cent sure they were being made a fool of. The laughs, when they returned to their boss sheepishly, always stung a little, but this kind of light humour was also a sign of inclusivity and team building. A clear message was being sent to everyone in the group: *We're a team, we're here to work hard, but we'll have fun too . . . And no one is immune from the pranks.* Once I'd shaken off my newbie wings, I soon enjoyed ribbing the fresh recruits as much as my elders had enjoyed ribbing me during my arrival. It wasn't bullying – far from it, in fact. I wanted them to feel welcome. Soon, I was involved in the thick of the action.

Part of every firefighter's working month involved night-shift work. That's where a watch would be on duty at the station throughout the twilight hours. Of course, this line of duty comes in for a little stick from the other emergency services. Yes, we have bunks and, yes, we'll sleep through the night if the bells don't go down at any point. However, we'll also leap into action at the first sign of trouble. It's also worth pointing out that we're not paid any extra salary for those night shifts and there are certainly no bonuses on offer. Meanwhile, provided they hit their hourly quota, the Ambulance services get a 25 per cent unsociable hours pay increment. The men and women of the Fire Service aren't afforded that financial uplift. Once our training, maintenance and administrative duties are complete, we'll bed down for the night. That's if no one from the watch is a rowdy, mouth-breathing snorer – which is a rare occurrence!

Like the occasion a watch was asked to send a firefighter on an 'out duty' – a process that happens whenever a fire station elsewhere is short on numbers, due to leave or sickness. In those cases, another station has to provide a member of their team for a shift and nine times out of ten, in days gone by, the newbie would be tasked with going. The chosen firefighter then took their own vehicle to the station in question, taking their PPE, bedding and personals with them, at which point, anyone not wise to the type of fun and games that went on within the Fire Service then, could expect some sort of shenanigans.

I heard a story once about a firefighter being sent on an 'out duty'. The station that was asked dispatched their newest face. But there was a catch.

'Son, you'll have to take your own mattress to the other station,' said the officer, somehow keeping a straight face.

'What?' said the newbie, looking confused. 'Where am I going to get that from?'

'Upstairs. Just squeeze one into your car and drive over. Don't worry, this happens all the time.'

Except it never did, and as the entire watch gathered round the window overlooking the car park, it was impossible not to laugh as he pushed and folded and twisted a way-too-big mattress into the back of his way-too-small car. When it had been fixed in place, the doors and windows of his vehicle looked set to burst, and by the time he'd made it to his location, word had already reached them. Their firefighting guest for the evening had fallen for the age old 'take a mattress with you' gag.

He strolled into the appliance bay with his personals and PPE, dragging the bulky mattress behind him.

'You're new to the job, aren't you, fella ?' said the officer-in-charge upon spotting this guy entering his station.

The newbie nodded. 'Yes Guv, how do you know that ?'

'Because there's plenty of mattresses upstairs in the dorm, you doughnut ! You've been had. But seeing as you're on your feet, can you pop down to the breathing apparatus servicing room and ask one of my lot for a left-handed screwdriver please ?'

By then, the game was up, though. Like my experience with the dishwasher, a lesson had been learned: *Firefighters are very often wind-up merchants.* Like everyone before him, that had ever squeezed a mattress into their car, there was no way that new face going to let his guard down again.

Through my early years I became well versed in the art of the wind-up, mostly spotting them, but learned that an effective tool in a firefighter's armoury turned out to be the office printer. This was particularly handy when creating official-looking (but definitely not official) documents. And a favourite wind-up of the watch would be to ask the latest probationary firefighter out to the foot of the drill tower to check the radiation levels above it. It was here that the telecommunication masts at a fire station were positioned. Waving a self-made document around, which featured a space for dates, times and radiation signal readings, the newest member was instructed to go outside to point a radiation survey meter towards the aerials. They were to note any readings they might have registered into a book. The paperwork was very clear: each individual tasked with recording the radiation signals had to check the telecommunications masts every ten minutes for an hour, without fail, even if the weather resembled a meteorological warzone. He or she also had to ignore the very real possibility that their watchmates were sat in the warmth, sipping on hot teas and scoffing Chocolate Hobnobs.

A more advanced version of this stunt later involved yet another official-looking sheet of paper, though this time Fire Control were called into the prank. Our newbie had answered the watch-room phone one day and was told that there had been complaints from the local airport: the glowing red light affixed to our drill tower, in place to alert any low-flying planes to the high-rise building on their flight path, was malfunctioning. Someone would need to spend some time in the top floor of the tower (unless there was a 999 call, that was) in order to hold up a red lamp to every plane that passed overhead as it came in to land. Just about every victim registered the same look of confusion upon being sent to the top of the tower.

Is this real or a wind-up, or is this firefighting lark the weirdest job going?

Stuff like this was going on in brigades across the length and breadth of the UK and probably the most creative prank I'd ever heard involved an inner-city metropolitan fire station. It was the late nineties. A new face had arrived for his first day and by all accounts, after the initial introductions, the crew took a little time to hang out in the watch room following their daily parade, which takes place at the beginning of every work shift. Suddenly, someone noticed an odd-looking character on the CCTV system. He was wandering around the yard, uninvited. Dressed in what looked like a charity shop Parka coat, his thick-framed, NHS glasses were held together with gaffer tape and he was wearing suede moccasins, which, given it was a pissing wet February day, seemed a strange sartorial choice. If you can imagine a clichéd TV trainspotter, you'll be halfway to picturing his sense of style. As if his arrival hadn't been strange enough, the oddball then pulled out a camera and started taking photos of the two fire engines parked on the forecourt, still gleaming following their morning wash.

'Oh, bloody hell!' sighed the station officer, having noticed the arrival. 'It's that pain-in-the-arse, John! Just what we needed . . .' He sighed once more, turning to face his crew. *Who was going to deal with this public relations nightmare?* There was a decision to be made and the answer was staring right back at him, nervously: The Young Kid, Ollie.

'Right, Ollie, welcome to the watch. You're new, so you're going to have to take this job on the chin.'

Ollie was ushered towards the CCTV images flickering on a telly.

'You see that guy out there?' continued the guvnor, pointing. 'His name's John, he's a local anorak, drops in from time to time, but he's completely harmless and a very nice man. He just likes taking pictures of the fire engines. Can you go out there and humour him for a bit?'

Ollie, obviously eager to please his new watch, nodded enthusiastically. 'Sure, no problem.'

There was a caveat, however. 'But don't let him go anywhere near the fire engines. *Understood?* Keep him at a safe distance.'

'Yeah, of course, guv,' said Ollie, enthusiastically. 'Consider it done.'

On the face of it, this was an easy task. *Just how hard could it be to handle the local anorak?* thought The Young Kid. John couldn't have been more than ten stone piss-wet through, and with those specs, he hardly looked the dangerous type. *This would be a doddle.*

'Hello sir, I'm Ollie,' he said, having eventually cornered the slightly shifty-looking visitor. The guvnor was right: John was a weirdo. There was something about him that didn't sit right.

'John,' said the intruder, thrusting out a grubby-looking hand. 'You're new here, aren't you, Ollie? I know everybody in this station.'

Ollie laughed nervously. 'Good to know! How can I help you, sir?'

'Well, I love fire engines. I've collected models of them since I was a kid. Would you mind if I take some photographs? I'm collecting pictures from all the stations in the area and by the looks of it, you've upgraded your wheels. And they've just been cleaned . . .'

Figuring no harm could come of a few snaps taken from what looked like a disposable camera, Ollie carefully guided the visitor around the station forecourt, pointing to some of the newer, more exciting features and updated gadgetry on the pumps, all the while maintaining a safe distance between the visitor and any potentially destructive equipment. But John wasn't satisfied. Pocketing his camera, he attempted to climb into the driver's seat on the nearest vehicle.

'Easy there, sir, you can't do that,' said Ollie, yanking at John's coat.

But John seemed taken aback. 'I've been to every fire station in the area and no one's had a problem with me sitting in the front seat before!'

'Yeah, but this isn't every other fire station . . |'

'I just want one picture,' said John, who wasn't giving up on his ambition so easily. 'You can take it really quickly on my camera for me and then I'll get out, I promise.'

Ollie glanced at the security cameras above the door, an awful realisation dawning upon him. Every move he made while negotiating what was now a delicate situation was being beamed into the watch room. His new boss and colleagues were sure to be glued to the screens. Given that a firefighter's role was very much a public-facing gig, his PR skills were surely being analysed too, so not wanting to look like a grumpy piece of work, he relented. Besides, John seemed like the harmless type. What's the worst that could happen? John settled in behind the steering wheel with a grin.

There's a worrying truth about a lot of people in my occupation: we've been known to lose stuff and break things. It's commonly said that if you were to put a firefighter into a padded cell with three mobile phones, he or she would mislay two of them and drop the third into a glass of water – accidentally, of course. This, sadly, is one of the ironies of a profession obsessed with health and safety, not to mention rigid personal administration. This was from a time long ago when the keys on most station appliances would be left in the ignition – no one wants to be hunting around for the keys to the fire station when a house blaze is kicking off on the other side of town. Clearly, John, a top-of-the-range nerd, had figured this out previously; there's every chance he might have attempted a stunt of this kind before and as poor Ollie wrestled with the finer intricacies of a Happy Snaps disposable camera, the engine door slammed shut. His heart sank. *Surely this wasn't happening?* But it was, and when Ollie glanced up, John had started the engine.

'Wait, sir—'

Too late. The fire engine was pulling out of the station. Seconds later it disappeared into the distance. Ollie freaked. Unexpectedly, he was up to his neck in it, his career very much in the balance – *and on day one.* Panicking, he rushed back into the station and into his guvnor's office.

'That bloke, John . . .' he stammered. 'He's only gone and stolen the water tender.'

His new family, who were in the mess watching *The Big Breakfast*, sipping tea and demolishing a pack of Digestives, rose to their feet in disbelief.

'What the fuck, Ollie?!' yelled the station officer. 'I told you not to let him anywhere near the fire engines!'

'I thought he was harmless. He told me that the other stations had let him do it.'

'Forget the other stations!' roared the station officer, reaching for the phone. 'Get out of my office! I've got to ring the police and report it. And shut the door on the way out!'

Ollie was in pieces. For what seemed like hours, but was probably only actually 20 minutes, he paced the appliance bay floor, flapping. *How could I have been so stupid? Was my career as a firefighting hero over before it had barely begun? And was John secretly a malevolent and manipulative crook in nerd's clothing? It seemed as good a disguise as any* . . . The answers to all these questions were about to blow into the bay. The thief had circled the block, parking the pump in the service yard behind the station. Casually, he walked back into the building, cool as you like, checked into the locker room, where he threw his anorak and charity shop glasses into a corner and changed into his duty uniform. Fully dressed, he then sidled up to Ollie and tapped him on the shoulder as the new recruit paced the floor, chewing his nails, fearing for his job.

'All right, Ollie? We haven't officially met,' said the thief. 'I'm John, you got my camera?'

As the truth of his all-too-unfortunate morning hit home, Ollie noticed the entire watch standing behind him, his station officer too and every single one of them was laughing their heads off. He had been well and truly rinsed.

'Welcome to the job, son.'

In the end, I didn't have to hold on for long at the second-worst posting in the Service. Dad had encouraged me to submit a transfer request. It couldn't have been more than a month after I'd started there. At first, I protested and told him to forget it – *I've only been here five minutes!* But he wasn't having it – he'd even written the memorandum himself.

'Leigh, if you don't ask, it'll take you two years to get off that station,' he said. 'And that's providing you've put a transfer request in somewhere already. So, go in and tell the officer-in-charge. If he doesn't like it, tell him

I've told you to do it.'

When I eventually moved stations a year or so later, it was to the same posting as Dad, though we were only allowed to work together if one of us was on overtime during the other's watch, a procedure that had everything to do with personal safety. I could understand that. The fear was that if it all went wrong during a shout, would a son or a father's professionalism go out the window? Would I become a liability if I went in there to rescue my dad, or vice versa? If that type of situation were to kick off, there was a probability that a station wouldn't just lose one firefighter, but two. I could understand the logic. But on the rare occasions when we were able to work alongside one another, the emotions felt intense. I was standing next to Dad, doing the job we both loved; the vocation I had heard all about from him as a little kid. There was a serendipitous beauty to it all, I felt a huge sense of pride and belonging. But before too long, I was creating stories of my own – both heroic and haunting.

9

Fire, Fire!

I attended more and more shouts. I put out more fires. I worked more road traffic collisions. I pulled more cats from trees (only joking). My experience grew, my confidence expanded until I felt bound to the other firefighters around me. From talking to my dad and grandad, it seems as if it was ever thus. And I would seek out my grandad to ask him how my experiences stacked up to his.

In those days, it was certainly no cakewalk. Whenever Grandad was called into an incident involving breathing apparatus, he had to pull on a suit that was more in tune with the kind of costumes you'd see in an old *Doctor Who* episode. The protective outfit was clunky and unwieldy (it can be pretty uncomfortable now). Meanwhile, the air supply – called a Proto set – was nothing more than a big valve placed in the mouth and designed to re-circulate pure oxygen through a CO_2-absorbing 'honeycomb', though I'm not entirely sure how effective the apparatus really was. The rest of the kit was even more down-at-heel. Firemen wore a simple set of goggles to protect their eyes.[1] To keep the smoke from being inhaled nasally, a clip was affixed to the nose. But besides their primitive Protective Personal Equipment (or PPE – an abbreviation we all became painfully aware of with the onset of Covid-19), there was very little to differentiate my grandad's day-to-day experience from that of the modern firefighter.

Like today, people started fires through misfortune, stupidity or malice. However, rather than worrying about a terrorist attack on the tube, or in a crowded railway station, Grandad was more stressed about the large number of unexploded bombs left over from The Blitz, many of which were still submerged by rubble, or buried in the ground. Back then, it wasn't uncommon to be called to a park or building site, where an old incendiary device had been accidentally clanged with a pickaxe or dug up by a dog. This was considered standard work back then because, typically, the public summoned the Fire Brigade to incidents whenever the police or ambulance services seemed unable to help, such as when a small kid got their head stuck between the iron railings of a fence, or Fido had sniffed out a highly explosive weapon of war.

By the sounds of it, the style of jokes and piss-taking were very much a part of firefighting life back then, particularly when calamity felt like it was just around the corner. And Grandad was no stranger to this. On one occasion, while serving as the officer-in-charge of an incident at a large seaport, he was required to deal with

---

1 Yes, that was the less-PC descriptive back then in those days. I'm assuming they also thought that women's bras would immediately catch fire if they went near a blaze!

a troubling but manageable blaze on the twelfth floor of a silo complex. As smoke and flames belched from the windows, time was running out. Without a swift and clear line of attack, the entire contents of the building would be ravaged. Once a couple of fire engines had arrived and my grandad had spoken to the site shift supervisor, it was decided that his watch should get to the source of the trouble straight away.

'Right, let's go up and see what's happening,' said Grandad, pulling together the small team of site workers in attendance. 'I'll need your eyes to tell me what's what and where to go once we're up there.'

The men stared at each other. 'I think it's best if we stay down here,' said one.

But Grandad wasn't having it. 'No, I'm the officer-in-charge and I need all of you to come up to the twelfth floor with us because you work here and you'll know the building better than any of us . . .'

Reluctantly, everybody piled into the lift and ascended through the first few floors of the building. Suddenly the pulleys and levers clunked noisily, then there was a jolt.

The lift was stuck – it had been overloaded.

'So, how do we get out of this one?' asked my grandad, stiffly. 'Is there an engineer on the ground who can get us out?'

There was a nervous cough in the corner. 'Yeah, there is,' said a voice. 'But it's me. And *you* insisted everybody get in with you because you were in charge . . .'

The lift, and its passengers, remained trapped for some time. That's until another member of the watch on the ground floor checked upon the whereabouts of his crew, having become concerned at the ridiculous amount of time that was being taken to assess a fairly simple fire. Once freed from the lift, word of Grandad's humiliation was soon passed among his station colleagues. If his lot were anything like my workmates, the embarrassment would have stuck with him for years!

But some things had changed and I was grateful for it. While working at the sharp end of the emergency services in the mid-twentieth century, there was no such thing as legislation or manufacturing standards. In those days, house furniture was often stuffed with toxic foam that ignited quickly and delivered a highly dangerous payload of cyanide gases. Fast forward seventy-odd years and building standards have improved as well.[2]

In recent decades, car manufacturing and design has also shifted its emphasis towards safety, as well as style and speed. Anyone involved in a road traffic collision during the 1950s could expect to wave goodbye to at least one limb in the fallout. Metal tended to twist and concertina horrifically in those dangerously out-dated cars. But it's also helped my generation of firefighters that the roads have been built to be safer, as have motorways. Meanwhile, the science of fire and our understanding of it has improved greatly too, and rather than having to gain knowledge through painful experience, the modern-day firefighter is able to step into a simulator to receive a hot education on the behaviour and consequences of

---

2 Though looking at the horror of the Grenfell Tower disaster of 2017, when seventy-two people lost their lives, you might well argue against that.

backdrafts and how best to avoid them.

But that's where the differences end. By the sounds of it, a lot of the emotions experienced by the firefighters of Grandad's generation still resonate today and he often told me about being called out to fires in the middle of the night. The lights would flicker on in the station; alarm bells clanged throughout the building. Everybody on duty was required to gather in the watch room as the details on the incident they were about to attend were read out. Once aboard their engine, the crew would ready themselves psychologically and physically for the call in a way that felt so familiar now. But having neared the address of the burning building, a huge glow clearly visible in the distance, their appliance was then flagged down to a crawling pace by a crowd of neighbours and concerned citizens, all of them gesticulating wildly to the smoke billowing ahead.

'Oh no, what's this?' the crew would think. 'Has there been another incident?'

Then some particularly bright spark would yell into the window: 'Over there! A house is on fire!'

It must have been hard not to become a bit sarcastic at that point.

So what you're telling me is that we're just here randomly driving about AND you have a fire?!

I know this because my dad would tell me the same story. Amazingly, I've experienced the situation on more occasions than I'd care to remember.[3]

---

3 I like to imagine the first caveman who learnt to make a fire was immediately followed by the first person to come and point at it to let him know it was on fire.

More and more, though, apart from the actual jobs, I came to understand the lesser-known rituals and habits of a Fire Service watch and some of them were pretty unexpected. For example, everybody seemed to love volleyball. Why, I'm not exactly sure. The ins and outs of how it came to be a car park sport at most stations – rather than, say, football – had been lost to time, but I found myself increasingly involved in the daily matches almost from the minute I'd started as a probationary fire-fighter. I figured, 'What harm could it do?' Guessing the physical activity would a) work as a nice team building exercise, and b) keep me light and physically fit enough to climb and descend ladders at speed throughout my career, I threw myself into the competitive atmosphere.

Running around at high speed, serving and spiking volleyballs all over the show, certainly helped to maintain a healthy waistline but it also caused its fair share of drama. Back in the day, before the time when successive govern-ments had cut back on everything in the Fire Service from engines to paper clips, each station was tended to by a designated cook. They were an integral part of the firefighting family and a big part of the watch dynamic. For years, we were blessed with a cook called Annie. More greasy spoon than cordon bleu, she was a great sport and very much part of the everyday piss-taking. So much so that when a stray volleyball shot landed in the open window of her car one summer's day, we decided to take advantage of her security oversight.

Every station has a Road Traffic Collision training area and it's usually occupied with a number of old cars, all of them donated by the local scrapyard. It's here that we like to keep our skills sharp and we constantly run through a number of Road Traffic Collision drills using the tools required to swiftly and effectively deal with all manner of twisted collisions. One such tool, albeit a very small one, is called a centre punch and it delivers a small, shattering blow to a pane of glass, such as a car window. When freeing a trapped driver, or passenger from a vehicle, a centre punch becomes a handy piece of kit and the procedure is made fairly tidy, thanks to a sheet of tacky film that we spread across the glass. Everything sticks to it. As a result, there's very little debris flying about once the centre punch has worked its magic. This is very helpful, especially if someone with open wounds has been pinned to one of the seats.

Given this was a training area, the nearby bin was usually full of broken car glass nuggets because not every car-cutting practice session ran without windows breaking. Sensing a prank, I grabbed a dustpan and made for it, scooping up a load of glass and tipping a little into the driver's seat and footwell. I sprinkled a little on the tarmac beneath Annie's door. Then I lowered the still-intact window down fully and shoved a little glass in and around the rubber edges. To anyone passing by, it would appear that the pane was smashed to tiny pieces. Popping the ball on top of the mess in the footwell, I gathered the watch around to detail the prank's second phase.

Right, here's what we're going to do . . .

Stony-faced, we walked up to the kitchen. Annie was stirring a huge pot of chilli con carne – it smelt fantastic.

'Er, Annie, there's been an accident,' I said, doing my best impression of a scolded puppy.

Her face dropped. 'What do you mean?'

'We were playing volleyball outside and—'

'You've dented my car, haven't you? What happened?'

Trying not to laugh, I said, 'No! It's not dented. But a window's been smashed.'

Annie slammed her spoon down with a bang. The hob was turned off (because fire station cooks understand the rules) and she stomped outside, pacing around her car in a fury, poking at the glass in the seat. At one point I thought she was going to puncture our ball, she was that annoyed.

'Are you lot stupid?' she shouted. 'How many times have I told you about playing your silly games in the car park? What am I going to do now?'

As scripted, another firefighter stepped in for the next step of our ruse. 'Here, Annie, my brother's a mechanic,' he said. 'We'll get him to take a look at it this afternoon, if you want? We'll all chip in to pay for it.'

And I couldn't help myself: 'Annie, the cost will depend on the type of window, though. Is it an electric one, or a wind-up?'

'It's an electric.'

'Are you sure it's not a wind-up?'

Annie fumed, oblivious to the bait I'd just thrown her: 'You can see the bloody buttons, you bellend! Just get me a booking at the garage and I'll take it down there.'

Phone calls were made. Our mechanic friend had been dialled in and was ready to go, and when Annie later drove several miles to the garage, she was given a semi-serious assessment.

'So, what happened here?' asked the mechanic.

'Well, the prats I work with – and I'm sorry, I know one of them is your brother – one of them smashed my window while dicking around in a game of volleyball.'

'OK, let's have a look at it. Is it an electric or a wind-up?'

'What is it with that bloody question?' snapped Annie. 'It's an electric! Everybody at the station kept asking that too.'

The mechanic smirked, gesturing towards the inside of the door panel. 'Oh, I think you'll find it's a wind-up. I need you to press that button.'

The penny dropped. Annie's face darkened. She pushed the control switch, her undamaged window gliding upwards with a whirr. Half an hour later, having returned to the station, she mentioned only one word to us as we carried on with our next game of volleyball: *Dickheads!* We then had to live off a batch of dry cheese rolls for the remainder of the shift, which was boring, but worth it.

The volleyball court wasn't just a bone of contention in my station yard, it had become a hot button topic in my dad's day too, though this was because of a particularly uptight fire station neighbour. Apparently, he'd been offended by the Anglo-Saxon language that ricocheted around during particularly feisty matches and would often ring in to complain. His mood was only soured further when it came to the summer months and his wife took to sunbathing in her bikini. For some reason, he became convinced that daytime watches were perving on her from the station car park. Clearly the bloke was paranoid – well, my dad says he was. I can't vouch 100 per cent for what was actually going on but after a few weeks, the neighbour called up to moan again.

'Listen, the industrial language is one thing,' he shouted to the officer-in-charge. 'But now your staff are leering at my wife when she sits in the garden.'

The officer-in-charge immediately apologised. He assured the gentleman that it was probably just a misunderstanding, but he would chat to the firefighters in question to clarify the situation.

The watch was none too pleased when the complaint was relayed.

'What's his fucking problem?' said one of my dad's mates. 'We're out there playing volleyball. No one gives a shit about what his wife is doing . . .'

They probably weren't impressed that the officer-in-charge hadn't backed them to the hilt either. All of which would explain what happened next.

Later that night, one of the watch went to the Road Traffic Collision training area and grabbed a drill dummy. Every station has at least one or two on the property and they're generally used to replicate the extraction of a casualty from a car, or for a house fire drill. Despite being heavy and cumbersome, they looked fairly realistic from a distance. They also made for effective comedy props and the watch decided to exact their revenge on both their paranoid neighbour and the officer-in-charge by placing the dummy on the flat roof of the station in a prone position. They then manoeuvred it in such a way that it looked as if it was staring into the nearby gardens. A pair of binoculars, gaffer-taped to its hands, only added to the impression that a peeping Tom was at work.

The following day, the neighbour called up with the hump. This time he wanted to speak to the station commander.

'Your lot are perverts!' he yelled. 'They're staring at my wife again, though they're now using bloody binoculars! What's wrong with them? There are specialist magazines they could look at instead, you know . . .'

The station commander became defensive: 'Sir, I can assure you that no firefighter here would do such a thing. You must be mistaken. And besides, they're all out just now, attending a house fire.'

'Oh yeah? Well, I can see one of them right this minute. He's looking straight at me from your roof.'

Confused, the station commander logged the complaint and when the officer-in-charge returned from the shout, he was despatched to the roof where the scene of the crime would have infuriated and impressed anyone stumbling across it. The drill dummy was still in its position, looking like a sniper's range finder, or, indeed, a pervert. Its binoculars were trained on a nearby garden, where an angry man could be seen gesticulating wildly. It didn't make for a pretty picture. Nor did the watch's apologies in the aftermath, which would have been delivered through gritted teeth – though at least everybody in the station would have scored brownie points for creativity.

There have been plenty of less imaginative pranks though. Under no circumstances should a firefighter ever disregard their fire gear and most notably their fire helmet. In many ways, firefighters should always consider it in the same way a soldier might treat their weapon. The first reason, from a personal perspective, was because a fire helmet was vital for our personal safety, particularly the visor. If something was to explode in a fire, or if a car battery burst and released an acidic, Jackson Pollock-style splatter across a watch member's face, there was every chance they might be blinded. The second reason was more to do with personal dignity.

During shouts we often use a Chinagraph – a thick black pencil used to write on plastic sheets and other hard surfaces (unsurprisingly, paper doesn't fare so well in extremely hot or wet conditions, so we use laminated white boards). But a Chinagraph is also an excellent tool in the hands of a creative spirit because any markings can be rubbed away with ease once the work is done and so if a Chinagraph was used on someone's personal property, such as an unattended helmet, any resulting vandalism was only ever temporary. During these moments of opportunity, the artist would draw a comedy face across the visor. They might daub a penis in the place where the nose would ordinarily be found. A pair of comedy glasses might make for an artistic flourish. The visor was then slid back into position so the owner wouldn't be made aware of their new-look image until it was too late. And not before the 'Pound Shop' Banksy had checked that his handiwork wouldn't impair the vision of the victim when the visor was used on the next shout.

Foolishly, I've left my helmet unattended once as an officer. The embarrassment I experienced afterwards meant I would never do it again.

We were called to a commercial van fire on a busy high street one summer's afternoon. Upon arrival, a well-developed blaze was in motion. The vehicle was popping and banging, giving the impression that it might blow at any moment. And almost immediately after assessing the scene, there was a loud explosion. The fuel tank had blown and I instinctively pulled down my visor to save my face from any burning material as I approached. Then I spotted an even more worrying sign: the first indication of an ages-old practical joke. Thick black Chinagraph marks had been scrawled around the mouth and nose areas on my visor.

Oh, no, I thought, *please don't let that be a cock and balls.*

But there was no time to check – I needed the protection and the fire needed to be extinguished. I noticed that a group of attending police officers were standing too close to the blaze for my liking and so I attempted to get them back to a position of safety. Some passers-by had also gathered at the scene and were taking pictures and it was important that I dealt with them, too.

'Ladies and gentlemen,' I shouted, 'can you all move back, please. It's for your own safety.'

I heard a snigger. A member of the public was laughing and gesturing to a friend to study my face. All of them could see whatever was daubed on my face visor and I was about to become a laughing stock.

I grabbed the copper nearest to me: 'So, tell me then, is it a cock and balls?'

He smiled and shook his head. 'No mate, but I wouldn't trust you with my email address.'

Later, job done, we drove back to the station, which was when I took some time to study the latest masterpiece. Everybody in the cab with me was laughing as I realised that some smart-arse had drawn a Venetian-style mask across my face in the style of the avatar most commonly associated with the hacking group, Anonymous. It looked great, but I felt stupid and I knew that I shouldn't have left my helmet unattended. But while the experience was humbling, I knew I'd soon get over it. This was yet another lesson to be learned and I took it to heart: always put your fire gear back on its peg between shifts; never leave a helmet on the floor in the appliance bay when another watch is on duty.

I promised myself never to do it again. With knowledge, and a Chinagraph, I had power. And there would be every chance to exact my revenge in the future.

10

Another Fine Mess

At the heart of the network of all the pranks, jokes and piss-taking, there is a sacred place. On the face of it, the dining room, or 'mess' as firefighters like to call it, is a room located on every fire station, where the watch will often gather during their shift. There's an industrial standard kitchen to cook in and stainless-steel shelves and cupboards stuffed with cooking utensils. Each watch gets their own cupboard and fridge. And there's a golden rule: *no stealing the biscuits.* Tables, chairs and a TV take up most of the room and during the day and night shifts, between drills, inspections and firecalls, the watch will generally gather in the mess to eat, drink tea, decompress and chat. When I say 'chat', I mean take the piss out of each other. But if an outsider were to spend more than five minutes in these rooms, they would understand very quickly that the mess represents something very important to firefighters: it's the heartbeat of any fire station.

In that one space, team camaraderie is defined not just for a period of months, or years, but generations. Gags that are prevalent today were knocking around when my grandad was putting out fires and the most common of these involves the sugar and salt, which look strangely similar from a distance. Whenever a watch changes over and the other watch is out on an overtime firecall, the mess room usually still occupies the contents of the off-going shift's cupboards. At the earliest opportunity, it's wise for the returning crew to conduct a taste test on their various condiments, sweeteners and seasonings at the start of their next shift, because you can guarantee some smart-arse will have filled the saltshakers with sugar and the sugar dispensers with salt. Often though, this is forgotten. The next time a brew is made and the watch sits down for a customary early cuppa, someone will groan loudly.

'Sack it off everybody, someone's fucked us on the sugar again!'

In recent years, the stakes have increased on switch-eroos of this kind, or, at least, they have in the fire station I've worked at. One particularly devious, and still unknown, individual has taken to swapping our supply of ready-salted peanuts for a brand seasoned with a seriously hot chilli spice. The problem is that, on sight, the two varieties of nut are indistinguishable from one another. Given the person responsible strikes every two or three weeks, it's also an easy trap to fall into – the watch is always given just enough time to forget. But when the perpetrator attacks, the impact is immediate. Someone will scarf down a handful of nuts without thinking. Then the burning begins, but no amount of spitting, or swearing, will douse the heat. Downing pints of water is ineffective, too. Within minutes, any remaining taste buds have been scorched to a crisp.

I'm sure these practical jokes are not solely confined to the Fire Service. In every mess hall up and down the country – in jobs where the stakes are high and the realities of helping the general public in challenging circumstances can be emotionally taxing – gags and practical jokes play an important role, as do nicknames. Though not the case now, a firefighter with the surname Woods would always be known as 'Chippy'. Likewise, Clarks are always referred to as 'Nobby', Whites as 'Chalky'. Others are more imaginative and usually focus on height, weight, hair, or some weird incident that might have happened at work. I heard of one bloke called Mike Shepherd, who was simply known as 'The Lord' – because 'The Lord is Mike Shepherd'. Everyone I have ever worked with takes their moniker with the humour with which it is intended. There are outliers though, as I found out to my cost one day when I was taking the family to Manchester to visit some tourist attractions.

One of the perks of the job is the fact that, as a firefighter, I can park my car in any station around the country, provided I phone and secure permission in advance. On this occasion, during a phone call, I was instructed to drop my car off at the most suitable location and present my Fire Service ID card.

'But you won't have any problems on the day,' said the voice on the other end of the line, 'Dinger's on duty—'

I thought I'd misheard at first. 'Hang on . . . *Dinger?*'

'Yeah, Dinger! D. I. N. G. E. R. He's the officer-in-charge. You'll have to ask for him by name though, otherwise whoever you bump into first might not know what you're talking about.'

Confident that everything had been squared away, I drove into Manchester. I found the station and then parked my car before asking the nearest firefighter for Dinger.

'Sure, I'll go get him,' they said, disappearing into the station.

A tall, severe-looking bloke was soon out to meet me. 'Can I help, sir?' he said.

'Yeah, Dinger?'

The officer's face darkened. 'I beg your pardon?'

'Dinger?' I repeated, unaware I'd been lured into a trap. 'I've been told to ask for someone called Dinger.'

There was a stony silence, then, 'I suppose someone thinks this is funny.' The officer looked down at my ID card. 'You, Firefighter Pickett, have been taken for a ride.'

I didn't know what to say. As far as I was concerned, I'd followed protocol to the letter. And then I happened to glance down at the officer's ID badge. My heart sank. The bloke's name . . .?

Station Officer Bell.

Oh, those fuckers, I thought, realising I'd been stitched up. Inwardly I cursed my own stupidity.

I took one look at his face and decided that now was really not the time to chance my luck by asking him to let me park my car there.[1]

After mumbling some apologies about visiting the wrong station, the door slammed shut and I was left to rue my naivety, not to mention a very costly day in

---

[1] Thinking about it, I may have overstated the global fraternity of firefighters a little bit.

exorbitant parking charges. After two and a half decades on the job, I'd let my guard down for a split second. But in the Fire Service that's all it takes for the opportunistic joker to pounce.

Before I get into the deeper psychological aspects of the mess and everything that goes on within, it might help you if I describe the environment and the kind of activities that are *supposed* to happen there. In theory, it's a space to eat and rest, though there can be impromptu trade union meetings and team bonding events, especially at Christmas, when a turkey dinner is usually rustled up. It's standard for every watch to have a designated cook, or a mess manager – an individual well-versed in burning the age-old classics of spaghetti bolognese, chilli con carne, chicken curry, lasagne and toad in the hole (if the watch was lucky). It's a thankless position, though. On payday, the mess manager will have the unenviable task of collecting a monthly fee from each of the watch. This is then spent on various ingredients and snacks. I've heard it said that it's easier to shepherd cats when the monthly collection takes place. As a result, the mess manager role is often given to the most patient personality on the team – Gordon Ramsay types are not tolerated.

The bells going down at dinnertime is one of the commonly accepted realities of the job. It tends to happen in those satisfying moments when the first lashings of piping-hot onion gravy have been poured onto a plate of bangers and mash. The collective reaction is always the same. Everybody groans and says 'Oh for fuck's sake!' There's a loud scraping of chairs as the entire watch, mess manager included, sprints to the appliance bay and an hour's preparation and cooking is ruined. Leaving a plate of food behind can be an emotional moment, but I'd rather eat a chilled lasagne on my return than have to crawl on my hands and knees through a burning building, a brick of pasta digesting slowly in my lower intestine – ascending a ladder with a full belly is not a fun experience.

When they do get to eat, a watch will religiously practise a number of domestic rituals. A particularly good meal (a rarity, sadly) will be eaten in silence until the plates have been cleared, at which point someone will inevitably burp loudly and declare, 'Well, that was a load of shit!' Firefighters are quick to take the piss. A critique of this kind is actually a backhanded compliment that says, 'It was amazing, chef.' Mostly though, the more important traditions of the mess are intrinsically linked to the organisation of household chores. The rules are simple and understood by all: it's the newbie's job to clean up and no amount of complaining or negotiating will shake up what is an institutionalised system. They'd be left for a couple of minutes doing it on their own before the watch join them, much to their relief.

Often the mess manager will be excused from any involvement in the tidying process as a thank you for their cooking efforts. But this can be a massive pain in the arse for anyone tasked with the washing-up and drying, because as any fan of *The Great British Bake Off* will attest: cooks are messy buggers. Also, it doesn't help that these moments are often ripe for piss-taking. I've lost count of the number of times a senior firefighter has offered to help a newbie in the sink by organising a conveyor belt system where the dirty plates are passed along in a line, dropped into the suds, washed, dried and then tidied away. Hunched over the sink, the probationary recruit is unaware that the clean plates are being passed sneakily back along the queue, where they're then dropped back into the sink again. After twenty minutes, during which time sixty plates will have been washed in what was a twelve-plate dinner, the high altitude penny drops and the victim finally realises they've been the butt of an age-old joke.

Despite these constants, some things have changed over the years – most notably, the introduction of women into the Fire Service. Back in the day, when Grandad was in the job, it would have been a very different story. In the forties and fifties, a backwards notion was still in play: the women stayed at home, the men went out and earned for the family. It was unheard of that the female in the house should act as the breadwinner – their responsibility was to raise the kids, cook the dinner and do the housework. The suggestion that a woman could work as a firefighter would have resulted in scorn and ridicule. And though Frank Bailey is widely cited as the first black firefighter in the UK, when he joined the Service in the mid-fifties, he was forced to leave after being passed over for promotion.

By the time Dad had joined up as a firefighter in the seventies, and once Josephine Reynolds had broken down those barriers as the UK's first female firefighter in 1982, a number of other women were applying to the Service. Sure, the enrolment uptake won't have been in the hundreds at that time, but enough females were at stations around the country for those people who believed that firefighting was exclusively a male pursuit to realise that it was time for the Service to catch up with the rest of society. Luckily, Dad has always been a liberal, open-minded bloke and he believed that having women in the Service was a great step forward. I'm sure there must have been a number of doubters, but they would have kept their mouths shut around him.

Even in the nineties, when I first joined, the Fire Service was struggling with its image. We were deemed institutionally racist and sexist across the board. And while you'd almost certainly have heard justifications and excuses back then about the proportion of applicants, what was certain was that the Fire Service wasn't representative of British society as a whole. Anyone walking into a station at that time would still have been greeted with almost exclusively one sort of face – that of a white bloke. And I'm absolutely sure that the culture of jokes and pranks felt very different if you weren't a white bloke. The Fire Service has not been immune from the same reckoning that most British institutions have faced, as we look at the past and find ourselves ashamed of some of it. As a white bloke myself, I'm certainly not the right person to say 'problem solved', but what I do know is that I've seen how the Service has worked hard to rectify that situation. Today, fire stations are a much better reflection of the communities they serve and feature a mixture of genders, faiths, sexualities and ethnic backgrounds, especially in the larger, multicultural cities, though there's always more that can be done and I know it is being done.

These improvements have turned the Service into a Swiss army knife, especially when it comes to dealing with community issues. My station serves areas that are very culturally diverse. It just makes sense for us to be a reflection of the communities we serve. Likewise, when a mother, sister or wife has been affected by an incident, one of the female firefighters nearby will step in to present a more accessible and empathetic position. This change is considered as an incredible asset in the fire appliance for the incident commander to utilise. Mainly though, it reflects a growing understanding of the role. The skill set of a fire-fighter is vast. We're capable of so many things – wearing breathing apparatus, cutting people from vehicles, water rescue and putting out fires – but if an individual, through their background, culture, faith, sexuality, upbringing, or their gender, can bring a little extra to the job, then it makes us stronger. A service that's more connected, empathetic and understanding towards its communities.

In my experience, firefighters are in the job to help the community they serve and it's a pretty selfless vocation. Ulterior motives don't go very far, and if I've worked with bigots, or individuals with closed-minded opinions, I've not heard them. Sexism, racism and homophobia are unwelcome and self-defeating traits in an organisa-tion with clearly defined moral values. Again, I won't pretend that my experience has been that of others, but I do know that there's something about the way we rely on each other, the way that any one of your watch could be called on to find you and drag you out of a burning building and vice versa, that fundamentally doesn't lend itself to discrimination.

Even with the banter, we make sure to check ourselves on any jokes, or language that might cause offence, and boundaries are established and respected. I've never seen an individual mock a protected characteristic of any firefighter. Respect towards sex, sexuality, religion and ethnicity is vital. No one is immune from the banter in the job but long gone are the days of nicknames based on your family heritage and things like that. After a settling-in period, it's soon established where a new firefighter stands on jokes: we discover their sense of humour, their character, and their hobbies (because we care). We'll hear all about their family life, their friends and their relationships, too (because we're nosey bastards!). They'll become a part of the day-to-day humour. Someone may booby-trap their locker with a water-filled wellie. Their tea may be spiked with salt. And they'll experience the special alchemy that occurs within the mess. There's a powerful sense of community that is created. Almost without realising it, you're bound into a kind of family. Those jokes and wind-ups act as a kind of therapy.

As I've said, there's a common understanding among people working at the frontline of human tragedy: it can be grim. Individuals operating within those roles are often exposed to emotionally turbulent experiences. They will see horrific injuries, play witness to life at its most brutal and survive fear and near-death events that will almost certainly scar them psychologically and in some cases physically. But taking the piss, or wallowing in a little gallows humour, during the fallout usually works as an emotional salve – it can take a little while though.

Of course, that doesn't mean laughing at everything. On some occasions, laughing or goofing around simply won't cut it. During those minutes and hours after a particularly gruesome incident, an eerie period of reflection will descend upon a watch. Sometimes that mood is only amplified by the duties we'll have to execute having returned to the station, such as scrubbing the pumps and equipment. I've been on calls where we've had to wash the equipment clean of blood and human remains. No one can just shake their head and get on with their day. There's a feeling, a mood that builds, and you feel it come back with you to the station.

Whatever *it* is.

In those moments, the very human reaction is to want to clean away the images from whatever's happened, or the experience, in the shower. But like all traumatic events in life, it can take a while for human suffering to leave the consciousness, if ever. The memories seem to lurk in the brain's peripheries for days and weeks on end until a natural processing takes place. That is, unless some long-term mental health trauma has occured.

Like most people working in the emergency services, I've also experienced my fair share of emotionally unsettling incidents. The heartbreak of a family losing their home, or the fires in which we've been unable to rescue the people trapped inside can weigh heavily on me, even though I know upset and trauma are a part of the job. Despite this knowledge and acceptance, some of the personal horrors I've experienced can still keep me awake at night.

That's because heavy emotions come at you fast in a fire. Yours. Those of people distraught at seeing their lives smoulder away in front of them. A family's horror and sense of helplessness knowing that a loved one, or a family pet, has died inside their home, and there's nothing that can be done to help. Within that psychological tumult, there can be distress among the victims, not to mention anger. Sometimes that rage is turned upon the emergency services trying to help, but emotions can affect the people working to put out the fire too. When my watch was called out to deal with a nasty woodland blaze that was burning near to a caravan park a few years back, what should have been a routine job turned into pandemonium for that very reason.

On paper, it was another late-night emergency. A stable shed had caught fire and it had spread to a forest area, but when I was ordered to send a message to our Fire Control via a fire appliance radio across the site compound, I heard a child screaming. When I located the noise, I found a boy. He was leaning over the body of a man. I rushed over and knelt down to check on his condition and vital signs – I could feel that he was still warm. Good news. The casualty still had a pulse, too. And the bad news: he'd collapsed between two caravans and there wasn't much space for me to work in. His face was also turning a worrying shade of purple and an asthma inhaler was clenched in his right hand. These signs told me he was going into respiratory arrest. A cardiac arrest would follow and he'd be dead shortly afterwards.

I radioed for help, but having called out, the precariousness of my situation hit home. No one could figure out my position because I couldn't describe it – I was caught between two caravans and the site was full of them. It was a bit like trying to find someone in a gigantic warehouse full of sofas. Luckily, a colleague ran by shortly afterwards and joined me, but by then, the man had gone into cardiac arrest. Our only option was to begin CPR.

The scene turned nasty. The boy was distressed, his emotions spiralling out of control. A number of families were gathering around us as we attempted resuscitation and there was some pushing and shoving as the mob became more agitated.

'You better save his dad!' yelled one man.

'Don't you let him die!' shouted another.

We were surrounded and intimidated. The mood had turned nasty and someone pushed me in the shoulder – God knows why. The brutal nature of CPR wasn't helping things either. From a distance the procedure looked invasive and violent, and because of the repetitive nature of what was an aggressive but life-saving chest compression, the victim's ribs were popping off from their sternum with a crack.

'One, two, three, four!'

CRACK!

Another bone split.

'One, two, three, four!'

CRACK!

Then another.

But nothing was happening. The man was close to passing. His skin had darkened and his stomach was releasing fluids into the lungs. I knew this because of a horrific tell-tale sign: every time I pressed into his chest, a jet of projectile vomit, a blast of yellow and green bile, splattered my hands, uniform and face. I couldn't avoid it. Within minutes, my colleague and I were covered in the stuff and the stench was horrendous, a stomach-bucking whiff.

Paramedics then arrived on the scene, but it was clear that nothing could be done. The crowd became enraged; their number had strengthened and it felt like all it would take would be one spark. Now the personal safety of the emergency services on scene was seemingly at risk.

'You've let him die, haven't you?' shouted the son, as firefighters formed a barrier around the body.

The medics worked on him for a further twenty minutes, even though everybody in the crew knew that the man had already passed and that there was nothing we could do to save him. But pronouncing him dead, there and then, felt like it could have been dangerous. We'd been intimidated and verbally threatened and our plan was to buy time until the police arrived to control the crowd. But really, the whole situation was messed-up. A man had died in gruesome circumstances. I'd been on my own for a while, exposed to threats and intimidation for the best part of ten minutes, surrounded by an angry mob. The trauma of this incident affected me for a while. Those stomach fluids would haunt me in flashbacks. Whenever that happened, I had to engage in something else, some forced distraction, anything to get those thoughts and that smell out of my head.

It's times like these that the safe space of a mess is vital. Somewhere a colleague can bring you a cup of tea, to sit with you if you seem like you want it, or leave you alone if you don't. To make a joke, or pass you the paper, or pat you on the back. Because they understand what you're going through – they've been there, or they know that one day it might be them.

It's in those moments that the mess and the camaraderie within it really comes into play. The bonds that have been formed through the humour and jokes now become a safety net of support, empathy and understanding. For this safety net to work, you need a shared frame of reference and that suddenly becomes true when you need their support. Every watch needs to be able to express themselves emotionally in order to move past any particularly harrowing events. These days, with more emphasis and conversation around mental health and wellbeing, firefighters are more empathetic and conscientious, and can often see the signs of emotional distress in colleagues among their rank and file. If those individuals need help and support, they'll be pointed in the direction of Occupational Health professionals for all the care they need. A lot of the men and women I've worked with have been quite open about their emotions and psychological wellbeing. No one is ribbed or judged for needing a helping hand – we care for one another and understand that it's OK not to be OK.

The fundamental notion of helping people is what links us all in the Fire Service, in a way I think is unique. The central reason for our existence is to risk our lives for strangers. There are plenty of other dangerous jobs where bravery is necessary. If you think about the military, that bond that exists between a unit during war. Their willingness to lay down their lives for each other. But they're almost certainly less likely to lose their lives running into a building to retrieve a group of civilians that may or may not be dead already. But if you were to scan through the list of deaths in the Service over the last twenty years, nearly all of them would have passed while trying to save the lives of people outside of the uniform. It's a unique facet of the job. Our role is to save anyone within a community, no judgements, no questions. It's a selfless existence.

And it's another reason why there is an unbreakable bond between firefighters, wherever they're working from, or whatever the character or background of the individuals on a station. On the face of it, that's quite weird. We're a mixed bunch; a lot of us mix like oil and water and there's an unusual and special dynamic on every watch. The majority of the people I've worked with have been great, there have been some I might have rubbed up the wrong way, and vice versa. But as a team we've worked well. Watches are generally a mixture of friends, colleagues and individuals that put up with each other during the working day/night and then forget about one another the minute they're off duty. But when it comes down to it, either in the middle of an emergency or in the quiet moments after a traumatic incident, they're always there for you.

If the shit was to hit the fan and I found myself in trouble during a dangerous 999 call, I guarantee each and every one of those annoying, sometimes intolerable people, who've pranked and farted and moaned their way through the day, would risk their life trying to save mine, if they had to. Nothing would be said about it afterwards. The response and the effort would be unspoken. It works across the board, too. In a scenario where another firefighter working overtime from another watch was trapped in a burning building, or unable to free themselves from a sketchy predicament, there wouldn't be any hesitation when trying to dig them out either. The Fire Service is a massive family and blood's thicker than water.

And it's a bond that stretches across geographic boundaries too. A firefighter understands that sacrifice. That's why whenever I've walked into a fire station anywhere in the world, I've been greeted like a long-returning family member. I get a kick out of it, because those meetings often feel like a personal test. It's as if I've wanted to check that the interpersonal bond truly, globally, exists. So, every time I visit a country, such as France, Spain, America, Cyprus, all over, I pop into a station whenever I can. I look into the eyes of the people who do the same job as me. I want to see if we're alike – *a person prepared to give their lives for others*. And I've never been let down; we're all the same. There's always been a great respect and connection with every firefighter I've ever met abroad, even if there's been a language barrier. The ID card comes out; the handshakes turn to hugs. Shortly afterwards I'm being offered a free parking space, a brew, lunch, an invite to a party later that day. I can't imagine many other occupations have that same, immediate connection between rank and file.

Back in the mess, you sit down, and you sip your tea. Three salts, just the way I like it.

I I

It's the Most Flammable
Time of the Year

In show business, they say you should never work with children or animals. However, I would like to amend that statement ever so slightly: *never work with children, animals or a large proportion of the general public.* All three categories contain characteristics that are irrational, quirky and downright odd. Though kids and dogs get a pass because, well, they're kids and dogs. The general public, on the other hand, have few excuses. What I've learnt over my twenty-plus-year career is that human beings have an astonishing ability to adapt to the time of year. Whatever high or holy day it is, they'll find a way to set something on fire or wedge something where it shouldn't go.

Spring cleaning

For a clearer understanding of how a proportion of the UK population can behave in an erratic and mind-boggling manner, let me tell you about the wally who decided to set his old shed alight – in situ, I might add – because he couldn't be bothered to drive to the nearest rubbish dump. The story begins on a balmy, midsummer's evening – the type of night most people would have chosen for an al fresco dinner. But sod that, because the Captain Sensible in this story had a fire to start. He did so by first emptying the shed contents into the garden. Twenty-five years' worth of paint stripper, lawnmower fuel, thinners and wood varnish had been stored inside, their fumes seasoning the wooden structure until it was an improvised, and unexpected, explosive device. He decided to kick-start the event by placing barbecue firelighters under the base, forgetting that a season of tinder-dry leaves was also packed underneath. Then he struck a match.

Whoosh!

Within seconds, his back garden was transformed into a street scene from the TV show *Peaky Blinders*. Flames belched into the sky. Plumes of thick, black smoke choked the air. And his fence, garden furniture and brand-new composite summerhouse started to melt and buckle under the intense heat. His wife and neighbours were unimpressed and, after a mad panic, the Fire Service were called, which was when things got weird. Having sped to the scene, lights and sirens wailing, we ran through the garden to discover that the shirtless shed owner had taken matters into his own hands. Despite his singed eyebrows and chest rug, and the nasty burns developing on his forearms and cheeks, he was manfully tackling a serious blaze with the type of hose one would only use to water the hanging baskets.

It doesn't take the Professor Brian Cox-type to work out that a domestic water supply is next to useless when fighting such a powerful event. In this case, peeing into the flames might have presented a more viable and effective option because the velocity of water generated by a garden hose is so weak. All domestic hose water pointed into the heart of a fire tends to evaporate before it's had a chance to do its work: the pressure and volume is pitiful. Unsurprisingly, as the garden burned around him, and the professionals got to work, our latest entry into the Darwin Awards was treated for minor burns and a severe case of earache from his wife and neighbours.[1]

Summer days

There are certain periods or dates in the calendar that generate more shouts than others. Bonfire Night, Christmas and bank holiday weekends are classic examples, all of which we'll get to later. But summer, as a season, can be a busy time for the emergency services because a) people love barbecues and b) the kids are away from school, they're bored and there's plenty of time in which to cause a little merry mayhem. I know because I was once one of those merry mayhem-causing kids, as we've discussed. In many ways, some of the work I've had to do since has almost certainly served as Karmic retribution.

I can understand the appeal of setting fire to the local cornfield when you're a ten year old, or gluing your hands to the handlebars of a bike for a dare. At that age, life is about exploration, risk-taking and breaking the rules. And

---

1 Safety tip: there are very few scenarios where lighting a fire is the solution. Be sensible. Break it up and recycle it at your local centre.

kids are kids: *they're supposed to make bad decisions*. But barbecues feel as if they should be an avoidable hazard because, in theory, the grown-ups are in charge. Though if you're to gather one takeaway from this book, it's that grown-ups make bad decisions too.

OK, picture the scene: you're at a friend's barbecue. It's a typical August day. The clouds are threatening to rain, wasps are running rampant and the Strongbow is lukewarm. The host has a new garden to show off. He's maxed out his credit card at B&Q. *Ooh, fancy!* And having started up his flashy new grill, he's decided to give his guests a guided tour. *Nice touch.* But, of course, there's a problem. The barbecue has been positioned way too close to a freshly creosoted fence. Meanwhile, the heat from the grill is radiating into the wooden panels, the wood is getting hot. Suddenly, in the blink of an eye, a panel is ablaze. Before anyone can notice, the next one has caught too, then the next. The flames soon advance along the fence like a line of toppling dominoes. Within minutes, the Fire Brigade has been called and the day is ruined – this can happen on an almost-weekly basis.[2]

Dealing with groups of anarchic kids often comes as a relief after a barbecue fire. At the very least, there's usually a slapstick subplot to take in. I once had to free a boy whose head became wedged between a set of iron railings, having tripped and fallen awkwardly while playing football (*Tottenham, sign him up!*). The velocity of his tumble caused him to become wedged between the

---

2 Safety Tip: When positioning your barbecue in your garden, leave a safe distance around it. You'll be surprised how much radiates off one.

metal bars, but he couldn't release himself – his bonce was too big. On arrival, I was struck by two thoughts:

1) This is truly a wonder of physics. How is his nut small enough to get in, but too big to come out?[3]
2) So, this really does happen? Better watch out for any discarded banana skins on my way home tonight.

Afterwards, we freed the unfortunate victim from his temporary prison with care, making sure that any passing jokers went easy on the piss-taking. But those incidents are forgivable because they're accidental – no one sets out to get stuck in a railed fence. However, less sympathy is extended to anyone caught in a similar situation through stupidity. If you've found yourself chained to a lamp post on a stag night, you should choose your friends more wisely. Any small-time criminal trapped in a smart car, having tried to break into it in the first place, deserves everything they get. And if it's a teenager who's decided to squeeze into a kiddies' swing and finds they're too big to get out, the rinsing they'll receive on Snapchat, Instagram and Facebook Live in the fallout can be nothing short of educational (Lesson #1: next time, don't be a bellend).

The most impressive reaction during such an incident takes place when the trapped kid spots the approaching hydraulic equipment required to break them free. It's always an intimidating piece of kit, complete with its

---

3 Absent-mindedly, I wondered if it was some sort of ship-in-a-bottle scenario and they'd pulled his ears back out with threads once his head had made it through.

heavy power pack and serrated blades, the kind that wouldn't look out of place in a *Saw* movie. At times, they'll freak out, or have a wobble.

What you gonna do with that, mate?

We'll wind them up for being so dumb in the first place. *We're going to have to cut your legs off – how else do you think we're going to free you?* His or her mates will film their every reaction as the teeth cut into the metal, grinding and creaking. There can be tears and meltdowns, but afterwards laughter, once the prisoner has been returned to the wild, they'll almost always want to keep a chunk of the twisted metal as a memento of their bone-headed decision. I suppose if you're going to humiliate yourself on social media so readily, you might as well own it.

But parents can be equally short-sighted once the schools have broken up. A number of bank holiday weekends dot the calendar throughout spring and summer, and a confusing percentage of people will happily swap the stresses of work for stresses of DIY home improvements – and sometimes they'll find themselves stuck up a tree. In one household I was called to, the watch discovered the visual answer to an age-old question: what does the unluckiest man in the world look like? Stuck in the branches of a towering oak, twenty feet up, was that very individual. In classic fashion he'd cut the branches around him so drastically that climbing down to his ladder was impossible. Though he'd made a concerted effort at least. Having dangled his leg out in an attempt to hit the first rung, he'd managed to kick his escape route away. Then, while ringing his wife for assistance, the mobile phone had slipped from his fingers. Several hours later, an eagle-eyed neighbour had spotted his predicament and called us in.

DIY season

Even worse are the events that take place indoors, because more often than not they will involve fire. One common cause of a bank holiday call-out is paint stripping, conducted with a heat gun (one that should arrive wrapped in fluorescent warning tape, screaming, 'Do not use!'). In theory, the gun is supposed to burn away the top layers of paint like a turbo-charged hairdryer and a lot of the time they do work. Sadly, though, I've seen the consequences of them working *too well*. The nozzle on a paint-stripper gun can throw out temperatures of a few hundred degrees, or more, causing the paint within its blast to bubble and liquefy. But the chemicals under fire are sometimes decades old, which is a recipe for disaster within an enclosed space. If that job has not been completed with the upmost care, sections of unintended woodwork can continue to bubble and smoulder for some time after the burning process has finished. And if the Handy Andy (or Sandy) in question turns away to make a cuppa, or leaves the house to run an errand, the timber can soon catch fire.

If they're lucky, a neighbour will spot the smoke and call the Fire Brigade. And if they're not so lucky, the blaze will rage for some time, until it's too late to salvage any possessions from the property. If they're of a similar mindset to our friend stuck in the tree, or Captain Sensible and his explosive shed, they'll probably have done something *really* stupid, such as ignoring the need for building insurance. Then they'll find themselves in a whole world of trouble.[4]

Remember, remember

Winter is coming. A phrase famously used to usher in the grisly arrival of death, eternal suffering and an army of axe-wielding undead in the TV show *Game of Thrones*. But firefighters will use the very same phrase to refer to two equally intimidating adversaries: Santa Claus and Guy Fawkes. The big man in a red suit is a particularly stubborn nemesis because of the fire hazards associated with candles, fairy lights and Christmas trees. Bonfire Night is a pain because for some reason an historic act of terrorism is currently still being celebrated by the British public, sometimes with cheap and highly explosive fireworks imported from the far east.

First things first: the very worst people for organising unsafe and reckless home fireworks parties can be firefighters themselves. I've lost count of the number of back-garden displays where the host has opened up an armoury of cardboard-based, surface-to-air missiles with the capability to knock out a low-flying aircraft. If the military-grade Catherine wheels aren't enough to put the fear of God into me, some of the more creative IEDs are. I've seen mates taping three or four rockets together, under the impression that the resulting light show will be

---

4 Safety tip: Take your time. It's not a flame thrower. It'll take a bit longer but you won't burn your house down. And make sure you have insurance, cause you never know when you might need it.

bigger, bolder and louder as a result. What they haven't realised is that fireworks are designed with velocity and height in mind. Weight and mass are very important when launching explosive powder into the air, so a heavy construct can struggle to make it above building height before detonating. How some of my mates haven't lost an eye or digit so far is beyond me.

I'm not sure why firefighters are so gung-ho when it comes to such events, though I suspect our devil-may-care worldview comes from a supposed ability to deal with the consequences. If something was to go wrong and a bonfire burned out of control, or a rocket careered into a shed full of lawnmower petrol, then who better to deal with it than the mob of giggling firefighters in attendance? One associate who will remain nameless even taped a handful of sparklers to a rocket at a party I once went to. Sparklers are metal-based and heavy, rockets have a limited amount of fuel. The firework sped into the air, reaching a height of around fifty feet, at which point it forked sharp left and exploded a few fences away. Panicked, the party ran into the street to check for any burning sheds or buildings, only to discover the doctored rocket had landed safely in a nearby garden.

Another firefighter who *will* be named in this book, due to his cavalier attitude to Bonfire Night, is none other than my dad, who when we were kids, once decided to up the ante at our annual celebration.

'Right, Leigh, it's going to be a big one, this Fireworks Night,' he announced proudly, setting out his box of pyrotechnics. 'I've made some of my own rockets with the powder from lots of other fireworks. I've stuffed them inside some cardboard tubing and stuck a thin bit of garden cane through the lot and taped it all together. If it works, it's going to make a very, very loud bang. You ready?'

My dad really was the coolest.

I buzzed with excitement.

That idea quickly evaporated when his homemade Saturn V spluttered its way over the roof and then slowly, but surely, began to submit to gravity. His massive blunder dawning on him almost immediately, Dad shoved Mum and us kids back into the house.

'Get inside, quick!' he yelled.

We ran for cover. Fortunately, the family was able to catch the percussive results of his experiment. A loud bang shook the house and at once, car alarms throughout the street were set off in a noisy whoop of protest.

'Oops!' said Dad sheepishly. 'I think we better stay in the house for a bit.'

As a firefighter, the shouts that tend to give me pause are the annual fireworks storage container blazes because they can be lethal, as everyone in the job knows only too well. In December 2006, two members of the East Sussex Fire & Rescue Service – Firefighter Geoff Wicker and Fire Service cameraman Brian Wembridge – were killed when an incident at the Festival Fireworks Ltd site at Marlie Farm, Shortgate caused a massive explosion. A large quantity of fireworks had been stored in a forty-foot unlicensed metal 'iso' container and a terrifying chain reaction event resulted in a huge detonation.

Ever since then, the Fire Service have been very cautious when dealing with buildings known to be storing large quantities of fireworks. That anxiety has only increased in recent years due to the huge number of cheap, imported products that tend to flood the market every year. Many of them have arrived from regions that aren't subjected to the same vigorous health and safety standards as those made in the UK and so they pack more of a punch. That's great news if you're only firing them over your house. But if they've been stored in their thousands within a warehouse and a fire begins, those bangers can become very scary, very quickly.

Some of my colleagues were called to an incident at a small industrial storage site while I was writing this book. They arrived at a yard to deal with a blaze, which, on the face of it, didn't seem particularly dangerous. However, they'd been told that the building also backed onto a storage facility packed full of metal iso containers, contents unknown. As they began dousing the flames, they heard a burst of nervous chatter over the radio comms. Apparently, some of the nearby containers had caught fire. Moments later, the conversations sounded more panicked. *Some of the containers were full of fireworks!* An emergency evacuation was ordered as the insides of two metal iso containers exploded in a series of deafening pops and bangs. A lucky escape.

There are laws in place to prevent this kind of incident from happening, but without casting aspersions on your typical fireworks-dealing entrepreneur, a number of the individuals involved in the business have been known to cut corners. Their attitude? 'I'm storing these rockets in a fucking great metal container in the middle of nowhere, what's the worst that could happen?' But when the worst *does* happen, that laissez-faire attitude is painfully exposed. Matters aren't helped by those involved in the import of dodgy fireworks. They can be very slow in coming forwards about the origin of their products, knowing they might be confiscated in a raid; they can also be reluctant to inform local fire stations about the contents of their burning building. Sadly, these shoddy practices have led to a loss of life. And if you're still unsure of the potential consequences of storing highly explosive materials in dangerous conditions, remind yourself of the tragedy in Beirut on 4 August 2020, when a warehouse known to be storing tonnes of ammonium nitrate caught fire. The resulting explosion rocked the city like a nuclear bomb, causing thousands of injuries and widespread damage.

Chestnuts roasting . . .

Less spectacular, but no less tragic are the events that can sometimes take place only at Christmas because they've involved highly flammable products such as trees, fake mistletoe and giant replicas of Rudolph the Red-Nosed Reindeer. The trouble begins when they're placed next to incredibly effective sources of heat, such as candles, cheap fairy lights and overloaded plug sockets. Really, when you think of it, the typical family Christmas environment contains more fuel than the average petrol station pump, so would you spark up a light while refuelling the car? *Of course you wouldn't.* So why is it fine to drape a daisy chain of five-quid fairy lights over a tree garnished with papier mâché decorations and surrounded with paper cards?[5] *Because it's Christmas and nothing bad ever happens*

---

5 Safety Tip: My advice is to never buy cheap Christmas lights. Always opt

at Christmas. Except, you only have to watch the festive *EastEnders* gloom-athon to realise that bad things *always* happen. People fall off roofs, couples decide to get divorced, and convoluted murder plots are exposed.

If it can happen to Shane Richie, it can happen to anyone.

When it comes to the most flammable time of the year, I tend to opt for safety. I like a reusable plastic tree because a real one can become tinder-box dry. There are a number of combustible oils and saps secreted by the wood and pine needles. If you think I'm overreacting, type the words 'Christmas tree fire videos' into any internet search engine, then tell me I'm making a meal of things. When it comes to decorations, I won't stand for any cheap electric lights either. And as for candles? Well, I like a woody aroma around the house as much as the next person: Malin + Goetze. Bolt + Star. Jo Malone. Sign me up for the smells, but not the flames, and much to my wife's annoyance, candles are banned in our house.[6] We've got three kids and the thought of

---

for a branded safety checked option. Also, check your lights thoroughly before use. If the cabling is damaged in any way, please dispose of them and buy new ones.

6 If I sound like a buzz-kill at this point, it's because sometimes that's my job. Just count yourself lucky you're not my wife or kids, and you don't have to take a holiday with me. The first thing I do on any family break is to check the safety protocols of the hotel. This process starts with the safety notice usually found on the back of the bedroom door. Ordinary people often spot these signs, ignore them and head straight for the minibar. Not me. Instead I'll read the paperwork from start to finish, before checking the smoke alarms, fire doors and extinguishers in a mini

them knocking a candle over gives me the shits!

One all-year-round product that really gives me the hump is tealights – those tiny pots of wonder and wax that arrive in little aluminium cups. They look nice and certainly create a nice vibe around the house if you position them along a hallway or mantlepiece. But boy, they're dangerous, exactly because of those cups. Like a cockroach, they can survive anything. I've been to the ashes of a house and found an unscathed tealight case in the midst of the bones of a one-time family home. The metal gets hot, but it doesn't degrade and so makes for an excellent heat source.

The most telling example of the damage a tealight can do was an incident when a semi-detached property was devastated in a blaze. Luckily, no one had died, but when a fire investigator later assessed the cause of the event, the officer approached the melted TV set to check if any faulty wiring had been the trigger point. Sifting through the blackened remains, he uncovered the tell-tale aluminium cup of a tealight. Holding it up to the occupant, he then did a little digging.

'Do you use tealights, sir?'

The house owner nodded. 'Yeah, I had one on top of the TV.'

The fire investigation officer said, 'In a glass?'

There was a sheepish shake of the head. 'No, we had

---

safety assessment, occasionally with some unfortunate soul from reception. Ignoring the groans of my despairing family, I'll then stride the corridors outside, pointing out the nearest exits and fire alarms just in case trouble kicks off. Only then can we party – I'm a right barrel of laughs, me.

it placed directly on top of the set.'

The signs were obvious.

'Well, sir, I think what happened here is that the tea-light aluminium has melted through the top of your TV, dropped into the guts of the box and set the lot alight. It's made quite a mess.'[7]

Thankfully, for every fire, or tealight-related disaster, some relief is delivered in the form of Father Christmas. Not the bloke you'll see gurning from the side of a well-known soft drinks bottle come September, but the portly, middle-aged volunteer cajoled into entertaining the neighbourhood kids for a bottle of cheap sherry. These selfless individuals are particularly troublesome if their CV mentions a background in am-dram. More often than not, they'll decide to make an appearance at the local shopping mall or toyshop. Sometimes, their attempt at a spectacular arrival ends in tears. Blokes get stuck on roofs, in trees and even at the top of a broken-down cherry picker. For them, and any traumatised kids in attendance, Christmas becomes memorable for a whole host of embarrassing reasons.

Given the frequency of these events, my watch was only too happy to help when one particularly adventurous Santa wannabe – employed by a well-known, northern European furniture store, which may or may not print the most infuriating building instructions – suggested turning the cliché on its head. Rather than becoming stuck at a great

---

7 Safety tip: candles can be perfectly safe if used properly. Make sure they're in an appropriate holder. Never have them under or near any curtains or drapes and never leave them unattended, especially with children nearby.

height, much to the horror of everyone watching nearby, this bloke wanted to create the impression that he was in a spot of bother, winding his audience up. To do so, he needed the assistance of someone with a whopping great hydraulic platform, which is where we came in. Handily, my watch was tasked with volunteering at the event anyway, though we were told to only arrive on Santa's instructions.

The scene was set. Santa had taken up his position on the store's roof, well in advance of any arriving families. Once a small group had gathered, he peered over the top and waved forlornly. All was not well.

'Ho, ho, ho, children!' he boomed. 'And ho, ho, ho, mums and dads!'

The crowd waved back excitedly.

'Well, everybody, it seems as if Christmas might be in jeopardy this year. Santa has got himself stuck on the roof . . .'

The kids started to look worried. Parents laughed nervously. *There was no chimney for Santa to climb down!* Was Christmas finished? Would Santa perish on the roof of this well-known furniture store, one that may, or may not, sell rather tasty meatballs in the customer restaurant?

'Also, my reindeers have flown home for their tea,' bellowed Santa, doing his best Brian Blessed impression. 'Could someone call the elves for help?'

There was a confused murmur among the parents in the crowd. Someone shouted, 'Elves? What are you on about, mate?'

'OK then, call the flippin' Fire Brigade, would you?' shouted Santa, keeping the pretence going with a few more over-exaggerated belly laughs and some hearty

Yuletide greetings.

At that exact moment, my fire engine moved into view, thanks to a text notification from the North Pole. We swooped in to save Father Christmas, lifting him off the roof with our hydraulic aerial platform. For a few moments, the bloke in the fat suit seemed to regret his elaborate prank idea. His voice got squeakier and his knees seemed to wobble as he climbed into the platform's cage. But once he was returned to safety, the drama soon created a celebratory atmosphere. *Christmas was saved! The Fire Service are heroes!* I made the most of our increased kudos by handing out a series of pamphlets detailing the dangers of tealights and pound shop fairy lights, eager not to waste a PR opportunity. In the glad-handing afterwards, the watch was presented with a free plastic Christmas tree by the store manager. Once it was positioned in the mess, we made sure not to hang any lights from it!

Like the other emergency services, professional footballers and the Queen, firefighters aren't generally that keen on working through Christmas, though we understand it's an important and worthwhile sacrifice. For the most part, we'll cross our fingers throughout the day for a quiet shift. Not because we don't want to do the work, but because we've seen the trauma caused by a festive blaze and it's horrible for everyone. The holiday spirit seems immediately incongruous once the presents have been scorched to a crisp. In the station, we'll eat a Christmas dinner, play games and try to recreate some of the holiday spirit. But not too much, because once the bells go down, anyone guilty of eating second portions will experience a bout of indigestion really quite quickly.

Generally, the incidents we're called to are fairly predictable. There aren't as many people on the roads so road traffic collisions are usually reduced in numbers. But, given that the majority of people are in their homes, drunk and eager to impress their relatives by serving flammable desserts in confined spaces, the most common shouts are for house fires – or at least the beginning of a house fire. The results can be traumatising when we arrive.

One year, we were called to a Christmas Day incident at a senior citizens' care home. My heart sank when the tip sheet came through.

A turkey has probably caught fire in the oven, or a joint of ham, I thought, sadly.

Two appliances were despatched to the location, blue lights glowing, but when we arrived a few minutes later, the care home manager was pacing around in the car park, fretfully.

'I'm so sorry!' she shouted, her hands up in apology. 'It's a false alarm. We burnt the turkey and set the smoke detector off . . .'

Typical! In community homes of this kind, a fire alarm system is often connected to a monitoring company, who will automatically call Fire Control at the first sign of trouble. This is designed to cut down on our response times. It also enables staff to concentrate on evacuating their slow-moving residents rather than stress about dialling 999. After all, every second counts.

'That's OK,' I said, 'I'm just glad it wasn't anything serious. Merry Christmas!'

But the care home manager wasn't done. 'Listen, if

you could come in and say hello, it would make their day. Some of them have been feeling a bit lonely . . .'

Sure, why not? I thought.

Myself and a few of the crew, happily taking it upon ourselves to do our bit for the ageing community on such an emotional day, walked into the home in our PPE. At first, we simply shook hands with the blokes in front of us and briefly swapped pleasantries and war stories (in their case, literally). But a strange energy was building in the room; I could sense something odd was going on. Call it intuition, my Spidey Senses, or a keen idea of impending disaster, but the hairs on the back of my neck were tingling. Then I realised why. A mob of ladies, immaculately dressed in cardigans and with blue-rinsed hairdos, had gathered behind us. At first, they seemed disinterested. They whispered among themselves and allowed the blokes to natter away freely. But it turned out to be a trap: my guard was down and within seconds, I was surrounded.

'Ooh, I do like a gentleman in uniform!' winked one as she grabbed my hand, her mouth that very specific shape when someone doesn't have their teeth in. For a split second, I worried she was actually drooling. 'You are a gentleman, aren't you?'

I wasn't quite sure what the best response would be in such a terrifying situation. Would admitting to a sense of chivalry only heighten her interest? Or, were Gladys and her gang about to intensify their attentions if I was to invent a rogue image for myself and answer with a firm 'no'?

'Er, I think so?' I stammered nervously.

'Good!' beamed the lady. 'Well, seeing as it's Christmas,

give us a kiss?'

I smiled – I already had a get-out plan. 'Well, for that to happen, I think you'll find it's traditional to have some mistletoe. And as a man of tradition, I won't be kissing anyone without some, so I'm very sorry, but—'

'Here you go, Gladys!' shouted a voice from behind me. When I looked, it was the care home manager dangling a clipping of plastic greenery in front of my face. 'No excuses now, eh?'

Seeking out an escape route, I looked to my lot. We had a newbie – this job was on him.

'Get over here, you!' I shouted across the room, pulling the recruit close as he arrived. 'This lot want a kiss under the mistletoe and you're the best-looking. Give them a merry Christmas!'

He stared at the wrinklies shuffling towards him, lips already puckering. The Christmas turkey was burnt and this particular old people's home were determined to feast.

'Oh, you've got to be kidding me?' he moaned.

'Listen,' I whispered conspiratorially, 'until you're not the newest recruit on the watch, these responsibilities fall on you. Now close your eyes and think of the Fire Brigade!'

To his credit, that lad gave one of the most impressive displays of selfless bravery I've ever seen. He puckered up for what seemed hours and endured all manner of tweaks and pinches on every set of cheeks he owned.

When booze and good times get together at Christmas, all sorts of weird and wonderful accidents can happen. But the very worst is the sozzled cook who leaves the house for a few moments. A gust of wind blows in and the door slams behind them. They're locked out. *And the turkey is still cooking inside.* Understandably, they don't want to burn the house down and so they'll call 999. We'll arrive at the property, break into the house with a number of specialised tools and then be on our way. *Merry Christmas, no harm done.* Sadly, over the years, a new frustration has emerged. Home occupants who find themselves locked out of their house or flat – when nothing is cooking in the house – have taken to calling the emergency services because they've been unwilling or unable to pay for a locksmith. To get around that problem, they'll then inform Fire Control that a turkey is reaching burning point in their kitchen.

But that's not what the Fire Service is for.

Sure, locksmiths are expensive, especially on Christmas Day. But dragging firefighters away from their primary roles is an immoral act. It also has the potential to cause some serious damage elsewhere. These days, I've attended all too many falsified call-outs not to recognise the signs of a bullshitter on arrival. They look nervous, then they feign surprise when we access the property – 'Oh,' they say, 'I could have sworn I'd put the oven on, basted the turkey and shoved it in the oven . . . silly me!'

It drives me crazy. On more than one occasion, I've called that particular person out, frustrated at the way in which they've wasted our time and resources.

'You knew all along your oven wasn't on, didn't you?' I said, after one job.

There was a sheepish shrug. 'You're right,' came the response. 'But I knew you wouldn't come if I didn't mention the possibility. And I really didn't want to have to pay for a locksmith.'

Contrast this with a little old lady I was required to help a few years back. One Christmas, we received a call that someone had been locked out of their flat. Mistakenly, I assumed the worst. It was someone pulling a fast one, I thought. But as we neared the incident location, more information filtered through on who and what we were dealing with. Apparently, a woman in her eighties was standing outside her front door, though she hadn't called us in. An eagle-eyed neighbour had spotted her shivering outside and shouted across. The woman, who was called Polly, wasn't wearing a coat and temperatures were hovering around the freezing mark. A 999 call was made.

When we arrived, the scene was even more heartbreaking. Polly was almost hypothermic and it turned out that she had accidentally locked herself out of the flat after putting some rubbish outside. Having realised what had happened, she attempted to call one of her children. As luck would have it, she had a mobile phone in her pinafore. She rang her daughter, but no one picked up – they were most likely eating their Christmas dinner.

'You've got a phone in your hand, why didn't you call us sooner?' I asked, as we let her back into the warmth of her home. 'You could have frozen to death out here.'

Polly shook her head. 'Oh no, I didn't want to do that! This wasn't an emergency and I didn't want to stop you from saving someone in far worse trouble than me . . .'

Since that moving moment, I've taken a more hardline approach when anyone calls the Fire Service on account of being locked out of their house. If I sense that they are trying to pull a fast one, I'll test their resolve by detailing the expensive costs that can be incurred in the event of a false alarm.

'Right, we can get you in, but only if your oven is on,' I'll say. 'If it's not, the entry damage will prove expensive because we'll have to use a door-breaker to smash our way in because you haven't left any windows open. So, I'll ask again, is the oven definitely on?'

A change of heart happens remarkably quickly if someone's been caught out in a potentially expensive lie. At times, it can take every ounce of Christmas spirit, not to mention my unswerving sense of moral duty, to stop myself speaking my mind.

Whatever the time of year, for every fire incident, there is a story. Some of them are tragic, others are heartwarming, which is probably not the best description given the subject matter. Then there are the escape acts, which seem to carry an element of downright good fortune. I was once involved in a freak incident where our fire appliance was driving back to the station when we were stopped by a bloke in the street waving frantically. Behind him, I could see that a car was on fire. Luckily for him, it was right place, right time, which was good news because he seemed on the verge of a breakdown.

Bloody hell, there must be someone inside, I thought. *He's in a right panic.*

We pulled up and the crew clicked into action. As we prepared to tackle the blaze, I grabbed the man by the arm: 'Is there someone inside, mate?'

He shook his head. 'Please, you've got to get inside.

There's a book in the glove box. Please get it out, it's very important, I can't lose it.'

My breathing apparatus (BA) crew, who were now equipped with the right gear to deal with the inferno, were briefed and tasked. After yanking open the door and leaning through the flames, they retrieved the leather-bound book from the interior. Thankfully it was in one piece, though it stank of smoke. Still, that was preferable to the owner losing it altogether. As we handed it over, the poor chap burst into tears.

'What's in the book, sir?' I asked. 'Why's it so important?'

'My dad left it to me when he died,' he explained. 'And it was my grandad's before that – it's been in the family forever.'

'It must be a hell of a story. What is it, an original Charles Dickens?'

There was a look of confusion. 'No, mate, it's an autograph book. It's got all the greats from the West Ham teams of the thirties, forties and fifties in there, right up to the modern day. All the 1966 England football team are in it, too.'

The bloke hugged me for what felt like minutes. Tears dampened my uniform. As an Arsenal fan, I couldn't help but wonder if I should have left it to smoke for a little bit longer.

What you realise over the years is that the memorable ones aside, so many incidents occur for the same reasons and follow a painfully familiar script. The most chilling stat about house fire fatalities is that the majority of them occur at night and in homes without a working smoke alarm. That one early-warning signal is often enough to get everybody to safety, while giving the Fire Brigade the time to arrive and act effectively. Elsewhere, lots of embankment fires on the motorway happen during the summer months because someone has flicked a cigarette away from their car window without thinking, or because the convex base of a discarded bottle has created the same 'magnifying glass effect' as that poor woman's crystal ornament. The generated heat then lights up the tinder-dry grass on the verge, choking the air and reducing visibility on the road.

Don't let anyone tell you otherwise: fire is relentless. It doesn't take a lot of encouragement to get going.

Probably my biggest frustration is attending fires caused by those carelessly discarded fag ends.[8] The most upsetting of these took place just a few years into my career when I was called out to rescue several pensioners who were sleeping through a care home inferno; a near-disaster in which a handful of gentlemen were trapped in their first-floor bedrooms, unaware that the structure around them was ablaze in what was really, really intense fire. On the ground floor, the nurses were panic-stricken. They knew that the corridor leading towards the men's bedrooms was now filled with smoke and there was nothing they could do to help. There was also a very real fear that the inhabitants might not wake from their sleep. It was my job to go into the bedrooms with my team and save

---

8 I look forward to the day when they're finally done away with and future generations can't believe they ever existed.

whoever was inside, but they were smoke-filled too, so time was of the essence. Unsure of the layout, we had to feel our way around through thick black plumes in every room.

Whenever we located someone in the dark, the scene was heartbreaking. In each room was a man, maybe eighty or ninety years of age, unaware of what was going on. They watched as my partner and I loomed into view, kitted out in a helmet and facemask, illuminating everything with a torch. It must have looked terrifying, as if we'd been beamed down from another planet. I can remember one frail old man looking up at me and whispering, 'Please don't take me away . . .' But there was no time to explain the situation. One of us grabbed his legs, the other his torso and we carried him out of the room as carefully as we could, past the fire that another BA team were dealing with, attempting to stop the flames taking over the corridor, our only exit route. At the stairwell, we handed him over to another crew, before stepping back into the corridor again – there was no messing about.

I think we saved around seven people that night. It was later discovered through a process of fire investigation that the blaze was most likely started by a cigarette extinguished into a glass ashtray. The ashtray had then fallen down the side of an armchair, but the cigarette hadn't been put out properly. It doesn't take a genius to work out what happened next.

Really, the most upsetting and predictable sentence that a firefighter hears in the aftermath of such destruction is this: 'I never expected this to happen to me.' Of course, no one does. You have a few drinks, arrive home half-cut and put a saucepan of baked beans on the hob. Moments later, you're asleep in the chair, snoring soundly and the contents of the pan are reducing down to chalky paste. Eventually, the contents become so dry that everything inside catches fire; the handle on the saucepan catches fire, any plastic, wood or fabric nearby catches too. If you're lucky, and there's a functioning smoke alarm in the house, you'll wake in just enough time to put out the flames. And if not, you could become another tragic statistic. Hopefully, someone dressed similarly to me will pull you out alive from the scorched remains of your home, leaving you to utter ruefully that fateful sentence, 'I never expected this to happen to me.'

Arsonists

Of course, some people want fires to start. Either out of malice, psychological instability or a need for a quick demolition, and there are plenty of characters who will happily set light to a property just to save a few quid. A lot of them get away with it too, which is probably why the concept of unwitnessed spontaneous combustion at a derelict building is a strangely common phenomenon. It's particularly frequent in rickety old structures, especially if they're positioned on sites that have recently received planning consent for some fancy new housing development.

Funny that.

Firefighters attend incidents like these all the time. An old, empty pub or warehouse goes up in smoke, but without any injuries or insurance claims (because who would be stupid enough to bring an investigation on themselves?) there's no hearing or inquest. The ashes are swept away and the sorry business is forgotten, which is far more convenient and cost-effective than bringing in a wrecking ball and a demolition team.

On some occasions an investigation team is brought in, though that's usually only when enough evidence has been spotted to suggest a fire was started deliberately. Handily, most firefighters are clued up when looking for telltale signals. In fact, all watch and crew commanders in the Fire Service have to work towards an accredited Level 2 award in Tier 1 Fire Investigation (FI). This enables them to determine in most instances how and where the fire began and whether or not there is anything suspicious about the blaze that requires deeper investigation. Think of Tier 1 FI as a slightly less cool version of Robert De Niro, aka Captain Donald 'Shadow' Rimgale, Inspector of Fire Investigation, from the 1991 Hollywood thriller, *Backdraft*.[9] One telltale sign of arson is the evidence of multiple seats of fire, which is an indication that the fire was deliberately set. And to keep us up to scratch on our skills, a yearly refresher takes place in which different fire scene scenarios are replicated through a number of controlled and recorded blazes. Among the mock events I have attended were a fire in a nail salon and a blaze in a little old lady's flat. For a full couple of days, the team investigates these staged

9 In fact, I should have made this clear right at the beginning. Please think of me as a younger, and slightly less cool, Robert De Niro the whole time you're reading the rest of this book.

scenes, scanning over the remains, looking for any clues as to what, or who might have caused the fire.

The FI team begins a fascinating and exhaustive process of elimination. We start outside, absorbing every available scrap of intel ahead, because the perpetrator might have thrown a lighter or petrol can into a nearby bush or bin. Once inside, we'll observe the behaviour of the blaze, looking for the initial cause and seats of fire as well as assessing the fire's intensity. After that, we'll check out any other factors surrounding the property and its owner. *Do they know anyone with the motive to do them harm? Has there been a similar event at the property before? Are there any signs of a break-in?* After a full day of analysis, our conclusions are presented to an assessor for critique and guidance. We also find out what actually happened.

In the event of a real fire, where we spot the signs of intent, we'll always secure the scene and pass our gathered intelligence on to those investigators above our pay grade, especially if we suspect it was an attack intended to endanger life. But it's not just on us to discover any clues of arson, we'll sometimes call upon our furry friends too. A lot of Fire Brigades have fire investigation dogs in their ranks, trained to smell out flammable fluids. When you see them in action, they're incredible! Each one arrives in Vibram-soled rescue boots, which are designed to protect the animal's paws from any sharp surfaces they might have to scamper over. Once they've detected a flammable liquid, they'll sit, obediently, demanding a treat. Elsewhere in the Service, we have other dogs to sniff out any individuals that might be trapped under the wreckage of a collapsed building. Some specialise in the breathing kind, others in the not-breathing. But each animal is on hand to help save the saveable lives of those poor sods messed up by the Square Triangle of Fire – the good, the bad and the downright foolish.

12

The Wheels of Fortune

Ask any firefighter what drew them to the job and pretty quickly, they'll talk about the fire engine. For many of us it's a formative memory – the sirens blaring, the lights flashing, the traffic parting for it.

Modern fire engines used by most Services are a serious piece of kit. And by serious, I mean they're big, unwieldy and very difficult to work with when manouvering in a tight spot. The pumps we use come in at a length of 8.2 metres and a height of 3.25 metres, so just under three times longer than a family car and over twice as high. I'm not entirely sure what the width was, but most engines could be aptly described as having the waistline of a Sherman tank. They're heavy too and any firefighter driving one was responsible for steering around sixteen tonnes of steel, rubber and aluminium ladders through a maze of narrow urban streets. As I would eventually learn, taking the wheel was not for the faint of heart.

To prepare for such a job requires some serious effort, though. I was a good few years into being a firefighter when I was asked to study for my LGV (Large Goods Vehicle) driving test and at first it was like being a nervous learner driver all over again. I redid my Highway Code and swotted up for a written exam. Once that was passed, I was tasked with taking the LGV course and for five days I worked with a training truck until I was well versed enough to attempt a driving test. Despite the size of the vehicles I was now driving, the format was exactly the same – it was possible to fail on either three minor mistakes in a similar catergory or one major. But luckily, I passed with flying colours and before too long, I was driving my colleagues to fires. My five-year-old self would have squealed deliriously – I know this because my twenty-something-year-old self did exactly the same thing.

With hindsight, my enthusiasm was misplaced because driving a fire engine soon proved to be quite a stress. At first, I was hassled by the rest of the watch during my early transits. The fun-filled comments usually started before I'd even turned the keys in the ignition. A bombardment of harmless humour would dog the start of my journeys.

'Leigh, just so you know, the accelerator is on the right – it makes you go faster.'

'How much room do you need? You can get a fire engine through there!'

The banter didn't last for long. Once I'd taken on my first few blue-light runs, driving at speed to a serious fire or two, the joking dissipated. Or maybe it hadn't. I'd been concentrating that hard at the time, it's highly likely I wouldn't have registered any jokes. Instead, on a blue light, I focused accurately on the road ahead, safely cruising over the speed limits when the streets in my area were clear, but sticking to them religiously whenever we were required to move through traffic. Strangely, I wasn't asked to do any proper blue-light training when I first started driving the engine. That only came into force a few years later, and like police officers in their high pursuit vehicles, I was required to learn the fine art of speeding towards an incident, lights flashing. It was great fun. Like *Fast & Furious 23*, but at fifty miles per hour and without the terrible clothes.

With the sirens wailing, I felt exhilarated. What I noticed almost immediately was that the traffic ahead of me almost always parted like the Red Sea. *Bloody hell!* I'd think. *Everyone's moving out of the way . . . for me.*

But the experience was nerve-racking too. My first serious call was to a man who had fallen from height on a gantry on a tower crane and I remember feeling really anxious as I got into the driver's seat. He had suffered life-changing spinal injuries and every second on the road counted. To calm myself, I remembered some advisory words I'd once heard from an officer-in-charge: 'Always drive to arrive.' In other words: *don't flippin' crash.*[1] Once I'd pulled up to the incident and the gentleman had been rescued, I puffed out a massive sigh of relief.

Thank god the first major one's out of the way, I thought. The other firefighters praised my drive and patted me on the back as they jumped aboard for the journey home.

Driving the pump soon created an extra frisson of excitement on every shout. Sure, there were some occasions where I'd find myself moving to an incident at a

---

1 Safety tip: adopt 'always drive to arrive' as your motto and teach it to the kids and grandkids too.

fairly relaxed speed. That sometimes happened if the location we were attending was a commercial building. Those places were often fitted with fire alarms – ones that tended to go off several times a month, usually whenever a worker made toast in the staff canteen. During those events, my speed remained steady; there was very little tension in the cab and 99 per cent of the time, the crew was stood down just as we were pulling into the property.

But there were some occasions where time was tight. I've driven to shouts when the printout in the station had made for grim reading: serious house fires where people had found themselves trapped inside the building. In those situations, the mood behind the wheel intensifies. My ability as a driver had to reach a higher standard because every second was vital and I'd find myself concentrating hard, in an almost trance-like state, passing through narrow gaps in the road at a higher speed than usual. On those drives, I'd make sure to present a more visible, audible and aggressive presence on the road. My sirens were blasted at full volume as I sent a message to everyone in the town around me:

Get out of the way, get over!

It's a huge responsibility to balance getting there quickly with getting there safely. And I would often find myself gripping the steering wheel so tightly, my knuckles would literally turn white and my hands would ache for hours afterwards. I wasn't concerned about my ability on the road, it was the unpredictability of the road users around me that gave me concern, and I soon discovered that the public could sometimes act quite recklessly when spotting a fire engine bearing down upon them in their rear-view mirror, sirens wailing. For the most part, the average driver would pull over, allowing the engine to pass quite easily. But I've also seen plenty of motorists freak out and panic, or worse, freeze on the spot and this can cause all sorts of problems. To avoid any nasty surprises, I always tried my best to give the cars around me plenty of time to react by creating a visible presence on the road. Often, I'd drive just outside of the middle line on the tarmac. I did this for two reasons: the first was so anyone travelling in the same direction could see my shiny red truck in their rear-view and side-view mirrors. The second was to alert anyone driving towards me that a bloody great fire engine was on an emergency call.

That wasn't necessarily a fail-safe technique. Despite the fact that even the most modest of family cars can outrun a fire engine from a standing start, the sight of our strobing blue lights was sometimes enough to cause a psychological meltdown. It wasn't uncommon for a driver to slam their foot on the brakes, skidding to a halt and nearly kick-starting a five-car pile-up. As a consequence, I'd have to slam on the brakes too, my unexpected emergency procedure launching bits of PPE, paperwork and breathing apparatus towards the windscreen as we screeched to a standstill.[2]

It was even more frustrating when two people pulled over at *exactly the same point in the road* – one on the left, the other on the right, effectively blocking any through route for the pump. An outside observer might reasonably conclude that the owners of both cars were mates

_____
2 Also, it wasn't so great if everybody had just eaten bangers and mash.

and they'd stopped for a chinwag. But for the crew on the road, desperate to extinguish a burning building several minutes away, it could take every ounce of patience not to launch a volley of abuse from all four windows. Instead, we'd offer the drivers around us a healthy slice of road wisdom as we passed, smiling and gesturing cheerily.

'In future, please take yourself away from the fire engine and find somewhere appropriate where you can park without causing us a delay.'

The firefighter's greatest nemesis, however, is The Smart Arse – the cocky racer with an unhealthy addiction to *Grand Theft Auto*. Upon seeing the engine coming up behind them, they usually pulled over sensibly in rush-hour traffic and then have a brainwave.

'*I know!*' they'd think. '*Everybody ahead of the truck is going to be moving out the way. If I get in the engine's slipstream, I'll be home in time for* The Chase.'

As an appliance driver, I used to see it a lot and the manoeuvre drove me potty. Mainly it bugged me because fire pumps really can't zip through town centres with impunity. We have to deal with speed bumps and pedestrian crossings like everybody else. That meant the benefits for any motorist moving tightly behind an appliance were minimal – they might cut a few minutes from their journey, but that was all. That was an insignificant amount of time in commuting terms, but for an attending watch en route to an incident, those minutes could be the difference between saving a life, or not. Trying to shave ten minutes off a commute simply isn't worth the risk.

A pursuing driver also increased the risk of an accident happening on the road. There were roundabouts and junctions for a speeding appliance to deal with. If the watch was lucky, they might not have to stop for a red light, or some bunched-up traffic. But even in a best-case scenario, their driver had to be 100 per cent switched on at all times.

They're thinking, *Is that old lady going to step out in front of me at that turn ahead?*

Or even, *Can I make the junction before that tractor pulls out in front of me?*

The last thing a driver needs is for some risk-taking herbert to appear in their wing mirrors, because it's already taking every ounce of concentration to reach a destination as quickly as possible. It's a massive headache to have to consider the motorist's safety in their rear, as well as the individuals ahead. On one occasion, I even pulled over in a fury to bollock the trailing motorist behind – I'd become that annoyed. We'd been speeding towards a house fire when the call came through for us to stand down. (Sometimes, if a number of pumps had been sent to the same address, the first on the scene might decide that only one was needed. Any other stations en route could then return to their respective patches.) Having been relieved, I switched off the blue lights at the traffic lights. Then I unbuckled my seat belt. Everybody around me knew I had the hump. The trailing driver had been up my arse for the whole journey and I'd been pushed to the limit.

'Where are you going?' asked the officer-in-charge. 'What are you doing?'

'I'll be back.'

I jumped down from the engine and approached the car behind. But when I saw the passengers, I had to do a double take. I'd been expecting to confront a flashy lad at the wheel. Instead, the driver was a young woman in her late teens or early twenties. That's not what caused me to pause, however. In the seat alongside her was a baby carrier and in it was an infant. The mother had been speeding along behind sixteen tonnes of fire engine, completely oblivious to the risks.

Oh my God, I thought, *what a selfish moron!*

Then I remembered my responsibilities as a member of the Fire Service. I had to be considerate and non-threatening, even though every part of me wanted to rant and rave. Most of all, I couldn't be offensive.

Which was a fucking shame.

The woman wound down her window and stared at me.

'Do you have any idea of how dangerous all this is?' I said, calmly, with consideration.

She shrugged. 'What do you mean?'

'Following us so closely through traffic at speed?'

The mother said nothing.

'Listen, it's incredibly distracting for the driver of a fire engine,' I continued, the pressure building inside. 'I had to stress about the cars ahead and what you might do behind me. You need to consider your actions more carefully, especially when you've got a baby in the car.'

'But I had to get my daughter to nursery on time, mate,' she said, completely oblivious to her own stupidity. 'We're late.'

I was lost for words. The woman was a road traffic collision waiting to happen, though she was clearly putting more than just herself in the firing line. She had a kid to think about too. Not for the first time I wished Doctor Death had been on hand with his chilling portfolio. Maybe then she might have comprehended the potential consequences of speeding so recklessly. Just one glimpse of those photographs would have been enough to change anyone's attitude towards road safety, even a top-of-the-range moron.[3]

If only the trouble starts and ends while an engine is on the move. Sadly, the reality for any appliance driver is that it can often begin once a watch has arrived at an incident, having cruised speedily, but safely, through a busy urban environment. Because no matter how hard you communicate the importance of common sense throughout the Highway Code, no matter how many road markings a local authority paints on the tarmac, someone will always park over the space reserved for a Fire Service pump, should it need to access the nearest fire hydrant. And don't think for a second that our appliances can function without one. Yes, some fire engines have the capacity to hold an amount of water, but the majority of incidents need a much larger supply. A working and accessible hydrant is obviously vital for a BA crew stepping inside a property fire. A continuous supply of water, plus knowledge and experience, is their only line of defence when dealing with a serious blaze.

---

3 Safety tip: I'm sure I don't need to say this to you but under no circumstances is it OK to tailgate any emergency service vehicle on a blue light. It's dangerous and distracting and likely to see you on a charge of dangerous driving.

If the water runs out for a BA team while in the thick of the battle, they're screwed.

The fire hydrant is such an important operational asset that a good officer-in-charge will alert everyone to the location of the nearest one as they arrive at an incident. Handily, they're nearly always surrounded by markings, which have been painted in bright canary yellow. Honestly, they're impossible to miss, but so many people do miss them, which makes me question the standards of optometry within the UK.

There have been shouts where we've pulled up at the right spot and seen, to our endless frustration, that some twat has parked over our closest hydrant. More infuriatingly, a perfectly good space can be seen just a few cars away. Often, we'll later learn that he, or she, has parked there for convenience. Apparently, it saved them all of fifteen seconds when arriving at their front door. More often than not, though, it's a neighbour's house being razed to the ground at the time, not theirs, and so someone else has to suffer for their selfish short-sightedness.

Not that the attending watches will stress too much for the thoughts and feelings of the inconsiderate. In some cases, drivers have been known to shunt a car aside with their bumper and the grunt of a sixteen-tonne appliance, especially when they know that one or more people are trapped in the blaze and it's the quickest and safest method of accessing a hydrant. In those instances, there isn't the time to conduct a door-to-door search for the owner. If you're selfish or careless enough to park over a fire hydrant, take note: you may receive an interesting paint job in the event of a nearby incident.

If that strong-arming procedure isn't available to a driver because of space, we'll happily smash a side window in order to lift the handbrake before pushing a vehicle away. Likewise, some lighter vehicles can simply be 'bumped' into a less inconvenient position. Small is beautiful after all.

Of course, the reaction to our desperate measures can be fairly predictable – and unpleasant too. The offending car owner, oblivious to the pumps, ladders and whopping great flames licking away at the furniture and fittings in their neighbour's home, starts demanding names and numbers in a fit of pique. They loudly announce that they'd quite like to see a head or two on a spike. It's then down to the officer-in-charge to explain the situation calmly and politely, pointing out that a number of lives were at stake and that the removal of the vehicle in question was necessary in order to save those lives, while preventing the fire from spreading through the community. But he'll receive a verbal thrashing for his troubles.

'Oh, that's fucking out of order!' yells the owner. 'I'm going to make sure you get the sack. I want your insurance details, too.'

Phone numbers are exchanged, details shared. And the officer-in-charge is congratulated by his watch for not giving his abuser a piece of his mind.

For some reason, the public can sometimes have a less-than-favourable attitude towards a fire engine on the move too, with its lights flashing and sirens blaring. The clichéd reaction to seeing a noisy appliance cutting its way through heavy evening traffic is to think, *Oh, yeah? It must be getting close to dinner time* . . . And this type of dismissive behaviour is only ramped up when the blue lights go on as a major event is about to kick off on the telly, such as the Champions League Final, or a decisive episode of *The Great British Bake Off*. But I'd like to cut down this particular urban myth, once and for all. A fire engine's sirens will never be activated in order to get back to the mess in time for a piping-hot dinner, or a TV special, tempting as that might seem at the time. God forbid, someone then hits a person, or another motorist on the road. There's really no justification for taking such a risk.

I can understand why the public might think we'd pull such a stunt. During a shout, I've made my way towards the front of a queue at the traffic lights, lights and sirens blazing. A line of cars has pulled over and made way. But having reached the head of the line, another call then comes through: *No further assistance required at this incident, you can stand down now*. I've switched off the siren and killed the lights. Then I've noticed the glares and looks of frustration from the drivers around me, all of them adding two and two together to make twenty-two. The assumption? I'd only made a noise to jump towards the front of the line. Sometimes the stares can be murderous. This is also relevant to other blue-light services.

If this ever happens to you, now you know.

There are always prangs and knocks when moving a vehicle as clumsy as a fire engine at speed. Many watches in the country will have a story about an appliance rolling over en route to the scene of an incident. The causes can range from poor judgement and bad weather and all manner of factors involved in having to move through traffic at speed.

If an accident involves a member of the public, then it's up to us make a quick shout on how to respond. The rules of the road are fairly clear when it comes to the Fire Service. If we have an accident en route, major or minor, we're duty-bound to stop but sometimes common sense comes into play. For example, if someone is injured, we'll always pull over to ensure that they receive the right care and attention until an ambulance arrives. The same applies if we're attending a relatively benign incident, such as a kid with his head stuck between the railings in a nearby park. In those instances, we'll alert Fire Control, who will then mobilise another crew to deal with the job. However, if we've only dented a motorist's wing, or knocked a mirror off while heading to a fire on the top floor of a block of burning flats, we'll apologise and speed on quickly – the priority always falls with those who need our help the most.

When it comes to minor bumps and scrapes, public sympathy should land on any watch driver at fault, because their colleagues will never, ever let them forget the dings. These days, my role in the Fire Service no longer involves driving an appliance but when I did, I was never involved in a crash with another moving vehicle. That was a combination of good co-ordination and good luck. Having said that, I've clipped wheel arches on brick piers and scraped bumpers, I've knocked off wing mirrors on parked cars now and again. A lot of the time, I relied on my watch mates to act as an extra pair of eyes, especially when I was trying to squeeze through a very tight spot. And if ever I pranged the engine, my lookout would shout one word, an announcement that chilled the blood: 'Cakes!'[4]

---

4   It'll make sense in the next chapter, I promise.

13

A Brief Interlude on Cakes

Long before I'd even joined the Fire Service the concept of 'Cakes' was already in place. I'm not even sure where it had first started. Some people think it began with the police, others the ambulance service, others the Fire Brigade. It doesn't really matter, because in the event of a minor accident, the unlucky driver was duty-bound to buy a round of cakes for the mess. In many ways, he or she was apologising to the crew for putting a dent in their vehicle. And by the way, they're not just any old cakes – a packet of Happy Shopper Party Cakes simply won't cut it. Fairy cakes are out, too. And don't even think about trying to get away with a packet of cupcakes from the local bakery. Instead, the psychologically bruised driver must dig a little deeper, forking out for boxes of cream-filled buns and éclairs drizzled in the finest Swiss chocolate and gold flakes. Being punished by Cakes can be a costly event.

The first time I was sent out on a Cakes-related punishment took place a few months after my first-ever blue-light event. I can't remember exactly what happened. Maybe I'd clipped a wall; I might have knocked something off the appliance as I passed a parked car. But having been told it

was my duty to perform a cake run for the watch, I soon
learned the value of what at first seemed a fairly arbitrary
punishment. Those fancy éclairs were astronomically priced!
I winced at the final bill as there were 17 firefighters on
my watch; my weekly beer money had taken a massive hit.

'You'll be a bit more careful next time, Pickett,'
laughed my officer-in-charge, having returned to the
station. 'You'll soon be broke if you're not!'

The inference was clear: Cakes wasn't just a tradition, it
was a learning curve, and I made sure to take care whenever
I was driving the engine. At the same time, my first round
of Cakes was also a reminder to be permanently on guard
around the other firefighters. Having set the boxes down
in the mess room, the watch gathered round. Everyone
chewed silently, the surest sign of a great cake. And then
one bloke picked up an éclair and pulled a funny face.

'Nah, I'm not eating that, it smells funny,' he said.

A lad nearby couldn't believe what he was hearing.
These were expensive cakes. *Surely it was because his senses
and palate hadn't been refined enough to appreciate their sweet,
creamy wonder . . .*

'Let me smell,' he said, leaning over towards the éclair.
'*Funny smell?* I'll be the judge of that!'

The firefighter put the cream-filled bun to his
colleague's nostrils. Another firefighter, in on the prank,
then pushed his head towards its soft exterior and the
impact smothered his nose, mouth and chin with cream,
chocolate and pastry.

Bloody hell! I thought. *How did you not see that coming?*

In many ways, I felt relieved to have spotted the
prank from a mile off, but the cost of that wasted éclair

smarted a little.

★

Over the years, Cakes happened from time to time, but not enough to nudge me towards bankruptcy. The reality about being a blue-light driver was that accidents, prangs, bumps and scrapes were an accepted occupational hazard. Pastries were bought on a two- or three-monthly basis and not all of the incidents were annoying – there was plenty of humour to balance out the frustration of denting a bumper. In fact, some incidents were so comical, they were later shared at messes around the brigade, often after an email detailing what happened had done the rounds. They were then retold at get-togethers across the UK until, eventually, they became legendary. The protagonist in a particularly embarrassing scrape could expect to achieve national notoriety, if not by name then certainly by action. Sometimes these events didn't even need to involve a fire engine.

One of these stories involved a station in the northeast of the country a good few years ago now. The story goes they had been called to a potentially nasty road traffic collision on a nearby stretch of motorway. A rapidly braking lorry had shunted into the back of a stationary vehicle and the driver was in a bad way. Having managed to climb out of the car, he then collapsed in agony, moments later. Worryingly, he was complaining of severe neck and back pain. As this was taking place, a guy from a national recovery company had stopped to help in what was his brand-spanking-new Volkswagen

Transporter – a fancy set of wheels recently entrusted to him by his employer. It was so showroom fresh, I doubt ten miles had been put on the clock. Everything gleamed on the inside, the hubcaps still sparkled.

As firefighters were making the vehicles safe, this recovery vehicle mechanic cared for the passenger until an ambulance crew arrived.

'Come and sit in my brand-new Volkswagen Transporter,' he may or may not have said. 'I'm going to sit behind you in the crew-cab seat and maintain your C-spine, because you really don't want to be standing up while waiting for the paramedics to arrive.'

This was an incredibly kind gesture and indicative of the type of outside-the-box thinking that often happens in the key worker sector. It was also extremely naive. Shortly afterwards, a paramedic arrived on the scene and assessed the patient as he waited in the brand-spanking-new vehicle. The diagnosis was grim.

'You have deformed C5 and C6 vertebrae,' said the paramedic. Then it got grimmer. 'You can't be moved,' he continued. 'We're going to have to get you onto a long board in situ to maintain the integrity of your spine. To do so, we'll need the Fire Brigade to cut the top off this vehicle.'

The watch drew in a sharp intake of breath.

But the diagnosis wasn't complete, there was time for a little reassuring humour: 'Don't worry, sir, you'll be perfectly safe. With the equipment they've got on that big red lorry, it'll peel it off like the lid on a can of soup and we'll have you out in no time.'

The mechanic was close by and heard everything. 'Seriously, it's a brand-new Volkswagen Transporter!

And there's only a few miles on the clock,' he wailed.

'I'm sorry, mate,' said the paramedic. 'There's no way around it. You really shouldn't have put him in your vehicle.'

'I'm so fucked!' said the mechanic. 'I'll be down the road with my P45 before the end of the day.'

Despite the £50,000 price tag on the Transporter, this was very much the right call. The injured motorist would have been paralysed from the neck down, had his C5 or C6 vertebrae damaged his spinal cord, and it was important to immobilise him as quickly as possible. The most secure way of doing so was to set him on that long board – a flat hard plastic structure fitted with a head block designed to prevent a patient from moving around too much.

The mechanic looked on, open-mouthed.

'Look, we're really sorry, mate,' said the officer in charge of the Fire Service (I'm sure trying his hardest not to grin).

The cutting began, fluorescent reflective paint flakes sprinkled on the tarmac around them.

By the time the patient was safely en route to the emergency room, word had filtered back to the seats of power within all first responder networks. A memorandum was emailed to everybody in the emergency services with a clear directive:

If an injured motorist has moved away from their vehicle, do NOT sit them in one of ours. You don't know what type of medical treatment will be required in the event of an injury being retrospectively discovered by medics.

I'm still unsure what action was taken against the Good Samaritan in the Volkswagen. But I do know one thing: if Cakes had been a punishment in his building, that poor sod would have been buying chocolate éclairs for the rest of his career.

★

Sometimes a round of Cakes doesn't quite make up for the damage, stress or embarrassment inflicted on a watch. I knew someone in another brigade who was once called to a fire on the motorway – an embankment was alight. The cause was most probably a cigarette butt flicked from a window, and in the wind and breeze created by a number of passing cars, all of them moving at high speed, it had travelled across the tarmac, the tip still smouldering away. Dry from a month without summer rain, the grass eventually caught light and the blaze licked its way along the hard shoulder for several miles. The passing traffic was being blinded by smoke, so the threat of a crash was severe.

The bells went down and they were called into action, appliances speeding to the scene. When they arrived, the fire was doused while the remaining hotspots were extinguished with the help of a chrome – a larger version of a farmer's pitchfork. These were used to shift smouldering grass around, so it could be soaked with water from an appliance hose. Just another method to assist firefighters with extinguishing a fire. The fire was put out, and the chrome cleaned and re-stowed to its place on the appliance roof. The traffic was able to move safely along the motorway and everyone was pleased with a job well done.

This event took place some time ago when a fire engine had space on the roof in which to stow most of its longer ancillary equipment. It was here that the main ladder could be found, the type used to tackle fires at height, such as on a block of flats. For the emergency service petrol heads among you, this space was also used to store a roof ladder, a triple extension ladder, two chromes, a ceiling hook and a stiff yard broom, because we don't like to leave too much of a mess behind. As the appliance cruised home along the motorway, my mate noticed the other vehicle from their station come alongside them. The crew was gesturing to the roof of the vehicle.

He assumed a ladder or something must have come loose on the roof.

So he said to the driver: 'Mate, pull over! Something's up.'

They pulled into the hard shoulder and the other appliance continued on.

'This doesn't look good, chaps,' he said as the watch clambered from their cab to assess whatever problem was awaiting them.

There's an event that dogs just about every touring rock band in the world. Midway through a gruelling UK jaunt, their tour bus pulls into a service station. As a hungover mob, the band go shopping for vital supplies, loading up on Rizlas, Scotch eggs and Haribos. Having clambered back into their seats, the bus pulls away and thirty minutes later, someone gets a phone call. *We've got to go back. Kev's been left behind.* But this kind of cock-up also happens to firefighters. Handily, we're a much more resilient bunch and the stranded party will usually try to chase down a vehicle pulling away from them at an incident. I know this because when my mate assessed the pump, he saw their very own version of 'Kev': a firefighter from the watch, still pinned to the engine roof, his limbs wrapped around the aluminium ladder. His knuckles were white and tears from the motorway windblast streamed his face.

'You bastards!' he laughed as he unpeeled himself. 'I'd just finished strapping the chrome down when you pulled away. All I could do was to hold onto the ladder. I've been motorway surfing since.' Then he looked crestfallen: 'But you know the worst bit? No one noticed I wasn't even in the cab.'

There was a mock groan of sympathy from the watch. No one was going to massage his ego in any way, nor were they going to forget that the driver had left a valuable member of the crew unaccounted for. The Fire Service, like the US Navy SEALs, operates on a simple code: no person left behind, especially when working on a motorway, several miles away from the nearest service station. For committing such a heinous crime, there was really only one reasonable form of punishment.

Cakes!

Fire engines have seen many design changes since then, one of which now prevents firefighters having to climb onto the roof for equipment. Perhaps too many cakes were being bought up and down the country for the same reason . . .

14

Cats Up Trees, People All Over the Place

Firefighters have very few adversaries. For the most part we're universally loved – or hen do's aside, at least ignored – by the public and other than a succession of those in charge of the budgets within governments, very few people have taken a pop at us, or our work, from the sidelines. Having said that, we do tend to skirmish with various sections of society from time to time, though any run-ins we might have generally border on the comical because they'll often involve domesticated animals. Most of the time the most terrifying nemesis a member of the Fire Service will have to face, outside of an actual fire, will be the household pet. Feral cats, blood-thirsty dogs and poorly thought-out animal choices – including snakes and poisonous spiders – can chill us as much as a raging inferno.

My very first encounter with the now-clichéd cat-up-a-tree event took place during my early months as a probationary firefighter when we were despatched to a house on Christmas Day. A feline had become stuck on a roof of a nearby house. The poor thing had been stuck up there for hours and it seemed pretty distressed, as was its owner, who was in a right tizz once we pulled up outside.

'Oh, please do something!' she wailed tearfully. 'Candy's my pride and joy, I'd hate it if anything was to happen to her at Christmas.'

Talk about guilt trip.

These days, we have very strict protocols when it comes to the rescue of animals trapped in precarious positions. If an animal of any description has been stranded for around twenty-four hours, we'll mobilise an officer to assess the situation. Accompanied sometimes by a member of the RSPCA, they'll make a judgement on how serious the welfare situation is for the animal and decide if it's safe enough for us to intervene the next day. No one resents the work – the majority of us in the Fire Service are animal lovers, even though we might accidentally run over the odd urban fox while racing towards a serious incident.[1] If, after forty-eight hours, the creature is still in the same spot, and we have the space to do so, we'll go up on an aerial platform or ladder to rescue it. Gone are the days when we'll despatch an appliance after only five minutes of a cat skittering around on the rooftops.

As I stood in this suburban garden, I looked up at the chimney stack where Candy was standing, I wondered, *How the hell are we going to get her down?*

Handily, my officer-in-charge had the answer: 'Righto, Leigh! You're the new boy, ladder off and up you go.'

---

1 That's not entirely a bad thing for the watch: an accident of that kind falls into the Cakes category.

Reluctantly, I climbed the ladder to the top rung-by-rung, painfully aware that the majority of the community was almost certainly sozzled and tucking into their hearty roast turkey dinners, topped off with all the trimmings. A slow, but steady drizzle of rain was gathering momentum and when I got to the guttering of the roof, Candy looked at me and mewled.

'Come on then,' I pleaded, making kissy noises. 'Come here . . .'

With a swish of her tail, Candy flashed me her arse and sashayed over the ridge to the other side of the roof. *The little shit!* Ice-cold water dripped off the back of my firefighter's helmet and trickled down my back.

'Guv, she's gone round the other side of the house!' I shouted. 'We'll have to take the ladder to the next street.'

What followed was a laborious process during which the ladder had to be taken down, carried through the property, into the back garden and then re-pitched against the guttering. I climbed to the top again, where Candy repeated her obnoxious arse-party trick. Up and over the ridge she went again. Piss-wet through, I was fuming. Not that the owner, hands wrapped round a fresh hot cup of tea, seemed too bothered.

'Thanks so much for doing this,' she said, as we took the ladder back through the house and into the front garden once more. 'I really appreciate it. And on Christmas Day too . . .'

For forty-five minutes, Candy gave me the runaround, by which point I must have climbed that ladder five or six times. The beloved pet did eventually make it to the ground through no work of mine though. Clearly bored of being the centre of attention, the little madam leapt around fifteen feet and landed gracefully on a flat-roofed garage next door, where, with a swish of the tail, she flashed her arse again and swaggered off like she owned the place, which she probably did.

Cats are annoying, but at least they're not dangerous. On more than one occasion, I've been called out to rescue a bird of prey and on getting the shout, I've initially felt excited at the encounter. Moments later, after I've come face to face with a set of razor-sharp talons, a beak that could slice off a digit or two and a terrifying, gimlet-eyed stare, my enthusiasm for the incident has faded.

Christ, I might get seriously hurt up here! I've thought, having untangled the sparrow hawk from a TV aerial. But once settled onto my glove, a position that would have felt comfortable for a trained bird of prey, everything soon settled down.

The strangest encounters tend to happen when a firefighter is required to enter a house unexpectedly. I visited one property in the nearby badlands in order to access a neighbour's property, which was going up in flames. When I walked in, I was struck by a stomach-churning stench. Fearful I might be stumbling into a *Line of Duty*-style crime scene, I felt instantly relieved having passed the bathroom and noticed the oddball menagerie inside. A tin bath was playing home to half a dozen live chickens, and staring at me dolefully was a donkey that had been tied to a table leg by a length of rope. The good news: I hadn't stumbled into a serial killer's house. The bad: I'd have to contact the RSPCA once the fire was under control. I think that might have been the only house I've ever been to where I felt compelled to wipe my feet *on the way out!*

On another occasion, I was tasked with conducting a fire safety inspection on a nearby block of flats. Part of that job involved checking the service rooms on each level – a 'consistent chamber' that runs from the ground floor to the very top and contains the building's services, such as the water mains, electric and gas meters. It's a fairly stress-free job, but while looking over the installed fire extinguishers and smoke alarms, I heard a nervous cough from behind me. When I turned around, a bloke was peering out of his front door nervously.

'All right, mate?' I said.

The bloke nodded. 'What are you doing, are you Pest Control?' he wanted to know.

'Oh no, we're firefighters from the local station. We're doing an inspection . . . Everything OK?'

'Yeah, kind of.'

'Kind of?'

'Well, you might want to be careful. I had a boa constrictor that got out of its vivarium and it's escaped from my flat. That was about two days ago and no one's seen it since. It won't bite, but you wouldn't want it to give you a squeeze . . .'

In an instant, our assessment started moving at light speed, the watch nervously scanning the nooks and crannies of the building. We never did find that snake, though we got the new recruit to open the doors and they nearly jumped out of their skin when we placed a long draught excluder quietly next to them.

Thankfully, I've never been injured by an animal while

rescuing it from a predicament, but I have feared for my limbs on one or two occasions, especially when dealing with dogs that might have been guarding a property. Weirdly, it's not the 'devil dogs' that are problematic. Mainly, Dobermans, Rottweilers and Alsatians are fairly easy to control. I find that crouching down low, taking off my hat and talking to an angry dog calmly is often enough to defuse any potentially nasty situations. In many ways, it's a bit like talking to a hammered Millwall fan. Instead it's the smaller, more yappy canines that cause the biggest issues and they don't come much smaller or yappier than the Jack Russell, AKA the little dog with the big mouth − the Napoleon of the kennel world.

Evidence for the case against Jack Russells would include the time I was once required to jump over a fence in order to access a burning property. I shinned over the gate while the watch waited for me to let them in from the other side, but before my feet had touched the ground, I heard the yap-yap-yap of a Jack Russell. When I looked down the garden, it was bearing down on me at full pelt, tongue lolling out the side of its head. Drool foamed around its bared teeth. I swear the eyes had turned a demonic shade of red.

'It's OK, little fella,' I said calmly, crouching down and taking off my helmet. 'I'm here to help . . .'

But the dog wasn't in a talkative mood. It certainly wasn't showing any signs of slowing down. And then I realised . . . *It was going to bite me.* And having assessed the situation, I did what any fearless public servant would do after being approached by a fast-moving dog, albeit a tiny one.

I leapt.

In one movement, I was up on the gate and squirming over the top, but I hadn't moved quickly enough. The dog jumped up at my trailing leg, bit into my calf and clamped down with its teeth, shaking its head in a furious death rattle.

AAAAAAAAGH!

Handily for me, fire-retardant clothing is made from a fairly robust material. Puncturing the fabric can be hard work, and though the Jack Russell's gnashers weren't able to tear into my flesh, its grip was still very painful. The beast was persistent too – it seemed to be clinging on for dear life. Luckily, with one or two flicks of the leg, I was able to shake it free. I scrambled over to the other side of the fence, where my watch was staring at me fretfully.

'Jesus! What's over there, a bloody Doberman?' asked one.

I shook my head. 'It's worse than that, mate – *it's Cujo.*'

When we jumped up onto the gate again to peer at the dog below, the little shit had parked its arse on the ground. It was staring up at us cheerily and its tail was wagging, like a model dog from a Pedigree Chum advert.

My officer-in-charge looked at me strangely.

'It's a fucking Jack Russell . . .'

I shrugged. My leg was in agony. What that tiny dog had lacked in size, it certainly made up for in enthusiasm (a lesson to us all, most probably). We made it through the gate into the garden in one piece and the watch got to work on the blaze. All the while, Cujo stared at my legs and salivated.

By the looks of things, I'd had a fortunate escape.

And it's not just cats and dogs.

We were once called to a garage on fire in the middle of a housing estate. The starting point had been a single unit in a row of around ten and it was crucial to get the fire under control before it spread to the adjacent garages, because who the hell knew what sort of petrol, paint and all manner of other flammables were stored inside. It was imperative to move quickly and protect the nearby properties from becoming part of a potentially lethal blaze. And when the first appliance arrived on the scene, one of the firefighters, Gary, grabbed the hose-reel and proceeded through a maze of back alleys to gain access to the garages behind. The rest of the crew provided support to him as they waited for reinforcements to arrive.

Then disaster struck: the water started to run out.

Gary started to flap a little. 'What's going on?' he thought. And when he radioed the pump operator, *nothing came back*. The officer-in-charge had heard the radio chatter and she went to investigate. So far, the crew had done a really good job of pushing the fire back. She knew that if the water supply wasn't reinstated pretty quickly there was every chance all the hard work getting the flames under control would be wasted.

'Something's up,' thought the officer-in-charge, 'I'll have to find out what's going on.'

She went off, back through the series of dark alleyways with her flashlight until there, next to a bright yellow fire hydrant, by a nearby pond, she spotted the pump operator (we'll call him Nick to save his blushes). He was on his hands and knees, his builder's bum delivering the second full moon of the night.

'Nick!' shouted the officer-in-charge. 'What are you doing? We're running out of water.'

Nick turned around sheepishly. 'I'm trying to get this frog . . .'

'A frog?!'

'Yeah,' said Nick brightly. 'There's one sat in this fire hydrant. Gary was only saying the other day that he wanted a frog for his pond, so I thought I'd surprise him with it.'

The officer-in-charge couldn't believe what she was hearing. 'Gary is on the other end of that hose-reel and if you don't get that water on pronto, he isn't going to be around to appreciate a bloody frog for his pond.'

God knows where Nick thought he was going to put the frog while the crew were putting out the blaze. Perhaps he was going to shove it in a pocket for later. And while this story is indicative of the love all firefighters have for animals, there's a time and a place for conservation, and it's not when a fire is burning nearby and a fellow firefighter needs that important element known as water.

But to be honest, the species of animal that gets itself into most trouble is homo sapiens.

We were once called to a house to free a man that had become trapped in his shower. I had to wonder what the hell had happened. *Perhaps the door had wedged shut and he needed us to release him? Or perhaps a ceiling or wall had collapsed leaving him pinned inside?* When we arrived the reality was far more bizarre than anything I could have possibly imagined: we were greeted by a woman who we were informed was the individual's carer, and having been shown up to the bathroom, we found an elderly gentleman, sitting in a shower hoist. A towel had been draped across his lap to preserve his modesty.

'He spends a lot of time in his wheelchair,' explained his carer, 'so we use the hoist whenever he has a shower . . .'

I walked over to assess the scene. 'Are you OK sir?' I asked.

The man smiled. He didn't seem in any pain. 'I'm stuck and it's my own fault,' he said.

I looked the hoist up and down, checking over the fittings in an attempt to figure out what had happened, but there was no indication that anything was keeping him on the hoist.

'Hmmmm,' I mumbled. 'I'm not sure what to make of this—'

'You need to look underneath,' said the carer from behind me.

Huh?

'You need to look underneath,' she repeated, pointing to the underside of the seat.

Taking a step back, I dropped to my hands and knees and peered upwards and my heart sank. *The poor sod.* In what was an unfortunate twist of fate, the flexible rubber seat was a 'waffle' design and some of the waffle had split. When the man had sat down, the split rubber flexed and opened and one of his knackers passed through the breach. It was now pinched and dangling through the seat. I winced. There looked to be no way to free him without the use of our tools – if you'll excuse the wording. After an hour or so of extremely delicate cutting with a Stanley knife and some nibblers, we were able to free the gentleman.

'I even saw the damaged seat and thought I shouldn't use it,' he chuckled as he carefully lowered himself back onto his wheelchair.[2]

Waffles at breakfast time haven't been the same since.

Or there was the time we were called to a fire in a hotel room in the early hours.

When we arrived the guests and staff were all out at the front of the hotel.

The fire was in a room on the top floor.

The officer-in-charge requested that I check the hotel accommodation floors beneath it to ensure no one had slept through the fire alarm.

A hotel manager gave me her digital master room key.

While firefighters tackled the blaze I swept the floors, knocking on doors and entering rooms as I went.

I became used to the rooms being empty, until I opened one door on the third floor. Not only were there people still in the room, but they were very distracted. Let's just say there were more than two people on the double bed.

Like rabbits in headlights they became motionless. Maybe thinking if they didn't move I wouldn't see them.

Remaining professional and unfazed I explained that the alarm that was sounding was in actual fact due to fire that had broken out in the hotel.

I requested they grabbed some clothes and shoes and followed me.

---

2 Safety tip: if something is defective and no longer fit for purpose, think twice, don't use it. Get it replaced.

Leaving the hotel lobby with them, there were lots of whispers from staff and guests. It didn't take a rocket scientist to work out what had been going on.[3]

Sometimes the situations people get themselves into are far less lighthearted though. Nothing causes my sphincter to tighten quite like a particular motorway smash a few years back. It had been a mission to even locate the vehicle initially. We patrolled up and down the stretch of road network the driver of the car described, but there was no sign of the vehicle anywhere. It had disappeared from view.

'You're in the right place,' said our Control. 'The driver says he can see the lights of your appliance and you're approaching him now.'

The point at which he'd left the carriageway had been located. Following a hole up through the undergrowth, we found a trail of destruction comprising a pathway of broken tree limbs and crushed ferns. Over the top of the embankment was the car. It had come to rest in a farmer's field on top of a Harris fence. The driver was stuck inside, but seemingly uninjured. When I got to the front of the car to assess the situation, I couldn't believe what I saw. The impact had caused one of the horizontal fence poles to shear away from the structure. It had been transformed into a razor-sharp wooden spear which had driven through the radiator and engine block, through the dashboard and passed through the steering

---

3 Top safety tip: It doesn't matter what you're doing, never be complacent when you hear a fire alarm sounding. Get out. Stay out.

wheel before piercing the driver's headrest, just above the driver's ear. If he had been an inch further to the left . . .

The only reason he hadn't been able to get himself out of the car was because the car's central locking had become jammed. After a brief period of cutting we were able to free him. He was unscathed.

'You are so lucky,' I said as I helped him away. 'You might want to think about popping into a newsagent on the way home . . .'

'What for?' said the man. 'Do you think this made the papers already?'

'No,' I said smiling. 'But you might want to buy yourself a Lottery ticket, because you might not think it right now, but you're a lucky winner!'

15

Power to the People

Because, as firefighters, we rely on each other, there's a sense of shared experience and common purpose among all of us. We know what we've all gone through and woe betide anyone who's not part of the family who sets out to attack us.[1] And that extends to our relationship with the powers that be. The more politically charged aspects of the Fire Service were thrust upon me almost from the minute I marched through the training centre's doors as a recruit. It must have been around week six or seven when I was introduced to the Fire Brigades Union (FBU), an institution long patronised by my dad, whose slogan at the time was 'Unity Is Strength'. For over a hundred years the FBU had been working as a check and a balance, helping to shape the Service in a myriad of ways as an integral part of the constant process of improvement that continues to this day. Over countless brews, Dad had explained how vital it was that I signed up. Trade union membership, he said, was an integral part of being a firefighter. Don't get me wrong, neither of us were troublemakers; disagreements and

---

1 That's *our* job!

rabble rousing were not family traits. But the importance of a healthy union in institutions such as the Fire Service was made explicitly clear to me for a number of reasons:

1) **Solidarity.** The Fire Brigades Union was a family, forty-four thousand strong at the time. My dad had been involved in the 1977 FBU strike – a bitter, all-out national dispute that lasted nine cold winter weeks. When the authorities finally relented, the Fire Service was rewarded with a livable wage and a reduction in working hours from fifty-six to forty-eight. These improvements in pay and working conditions would never have been achieved without the solidarity of an organised trade union.

2) **The Protection of Professional Terms and Conditions.** Successive governments had already eroded the pay and working practices of our country's most valued institutions, such as the NHS, the Police Force and our own Fire Service. As a result, the Fire Brigades Union has campaigned tirelessly to protect its members from further government cuts.

3) **A Voice.** The Fire Brigades Union ensured the voice of its members was heard at the highest level of government on issues of national importance, such as Fire Regulations and, more recently, the Grenfell Tower inquiry.

4) **Legal Assistance.** And if something went wrong, it was handy to have representation and a lawyer in your corner.

★

Having been convinced of their willingness to fight the good fight, I signed up with the FBU as soon as I had been introduced, collected my membership badge and flicked through an edition of *Firefighter Magazine* (a bi-monthly publication from the FBU), paying little thought to my newfound tribe. And then an industrial dispute kicked off a few weeks later. The dispute had been triggered by the announcement of a number of job losses within the Service. Battle lines were drawn. Eleventh-hour talks broke down. Dramatically, the Fire Brigades Union then balloted its members in my Brigade on what to do next and the decision was unanimous . . .

Strike.

I looked at the result and sighed: 'Oh, bollocks . . .'

I couldn't believe my luck. I was weeks into the job, not even out of the training centre, and still a little wet behind the ears. Thanks to my affiliation to the Union, I was also now involved in a headline-grabbing industrial dispute, the first in generations, where my colleagues would be visibly protesting outside fire stations. Then I remembered I was probably on fairly safe ground as a recruit firefighter.

You're a recruit, mate, I thought. *No one's expecting you to join the experienced socialists on the frontline of any demos. You'll be able to carry on with the pumps and ladders training and watch as everybody else takes to the streets.*

Speaking to a few of the new recruits, we were all of one mind. Probably not wise to rock the boat this early on. Best keep our heads down and not go full Che Guevara before we'd even celebrated our two-month anniversary in the job.

Then, on day one of the strike, my proud dad called: 'Son, we're going on a demonstration together.'

My heart sank. My dad had always been a political animal. He was a strong believer in the power of the unions and their importance in taking care of those in the Fire Service so they could take care of everyone else. The way he saw it, the reason people become firefighters is simply because they want to help people. Yes, there was job security, steady pay and a decent pension – not things to be sniffed at – but, to be frank, there were plenty of other jobs offering those things but which didn't involve your place of work being somewhere that's on fire. The simple fact is that firefighters care about their communities and the people within them, they want to provide a service. Dad understood the power of strength in numbers. Firefighters traditionally came from working-class backgrounds. In Dad's early years in the job, he'd observed the violent disputes between the National Union of Mineworkers (NUM) and the UK government. He'd seen first-hand the power of our union in 1977 and now I was going to learn about it too.

'But, Dad, I really think I should be . . .'

'No, this is important, Leigh. *You're going!*'

Somewhat reluctantly, I stood by his side the following day. I held banners and sang songs. It was a great experience and I saw the camaraderie and unity in action. Although I didn't think it possible, it made me love the institution a whole lot more. By the end of the day, I fully appreciated why my dad had wanted me to join him. I marked the experience down as a harmless, but interesting way to spend a day.

The next day, following several hours of scaling ladders and dousing flames in training school, the building tannoy squeaked into life.

'Firefighter Pickett,' announced a booming voice, 'can you come to the Commandant's office, immediately . . .'

Here we go again, I thought. *It's another wind-up for the new recruit. What will it be this time?*

But when I walked into the Commandant's office, something seemed a little off. The mood in the room was awkward. Worse, my training sub-officers were shaking their heads at me. The Commandant then picked up the latest edition of *Firefighter Magazine* and placed it face down on his desk.

'Pickett by name, picket by nature, eh?' he mused.

I had no idea what he was going on about and this didn't feel like a joke. I was a little on the back foot.

'Er, I'm not sure . . .'

'Do you believe in doing things in the right order?'

I nodded enthusiastically.

Had I messed up an exercise? Where was this going?

'So, would you agree that it makes sense to, I don't know, actually do a job for a bit before you lead a strike?'

'Well . . .?'

Then he turned the issue of *Firefighter Magazine* over.

I rotated my head so I could see the publication properly and stared in horror. The image on the cover featured a close-up photo of two blokes holding banners emblazoned with the words, 'Cuts Cost Lives'. One of those men was my dad, fist raised in the air, mid-shout, his passionate zeal clear to see. And the other . . . well, the other one was unmistakably me. I looked, if possible, even more passionate, even more committed to the cause.

Bugger!

'Oh!' I said.

'You dickhead! Wait till I see your old man,' he smirked and shook his head.

He waved me away and I made a mental note to stay out of his way for the next few days.

Firefighters don't want to strike, though a certain section of the national media would like to convince you otherwise.[2] But take it from me: when we do walk out, ninety-nine times out of a hundred, we're doing it because we believe it's the best way to protect the safety of ourselves and by extension our communities, because lives are at risk. The only option left in those circumstances is to take industrial action. We want the public to have the safest number of personnel, fire engines and fire stations. The irony is that to maintain strong and effective in those areas – *to protect our communities* – during industrial flashpoints, we have to put those same communities at risk by withdrawing our personnel, fire engines and fire stations from the frontline.

It's the age-old Catch-22 situation at work.

But what other option do we have? Over the years, it's become painfully obvious that the alternative to industrial action would be to say and do nothing. Taking that option could see Fire Service budgets cut year after year after year. That would only expose our communities even further in the long run, because once a trade union rolls

---

2 Often in large type, with very short words that begin with the same letter.

over by simply accepting the incoming financial attacks, it finds itself in a weakened position from then on. In my first months as a recruit, I learned that the Fire Brigades Union and the members within considered industrial action as a nuclear deterrent – it was a button to press only once all other options had been exhausted. And the fact was, it had been used successfully to protect working conditions and practices in the past.

No one enjoys the thought of standing on a picket line, though. One of the main reasons is because firefighters feel an element of guilt. The communities we protect contain our relatives, loved ones and friends. If someone was to leave the iron on at home, the metal scorching the fabric around it, the small flames catching on a tea towel dangling nearby, those flames then licking across the wooden cupboards in the kitchen, before building into a serious house fire . . . *who d'you think's going to run to the rescue?* The best people for the job are standing beside me at a demo. They're waving placards and descending upon Whitehall, blissfully unaware that somewhere a house is going up in flames. This is a risk shared by every firefighter around the country who takes industrial action. It's a hard decision to make for everyone involved.

Full disclosure: I *have* gone on strike in order to gain a fair pay rise in 2002 and in defence of my pension in 2013/14. But mainly, Fire Brigades Union firefighters make the decision to take industrial action when their position is that their conditions of service are in danger, leading to less protection for the general public, or they're prevented from doing the job to the best of their abilities, often through a financially mandated reduction in labour and/or resources. In other words: *cuts*. And over the last decade of austerity, like the NHS, the UK Armed Forces, the legal system, social workers, library workers, refuse collectors and the police, the Fire Service has been used as a political punch bag far too often.[3] As a union member and as someone on the frontline, I wish we lived in a world where there was more money for the Fire Service. But as a realist I understand that hard decisions have to be made by those in charge, especially as we face the next few years of economic uncertainty with the cost of Covid needing to be recovered.

The FBU have been vocal about their belief that the Fire Service is painfully under-resourced with fewer officers and less equipment. And it's undeniable that a succession of austerity-brandishing governments has cut spending, while piling on the pressure with our work-load. Nowhere is this issue more keenly highlighted than when discussing the issue of flooding and climate change.

In recent decades, this has become a serious cause for concern across the UK. Violent storms and rising water levels are a direct result of the climate crisis, as our weather has become increasingly unpredictable and savage. However, the resources for combating events of this kind are very limited. In fact, the government's answer for coping with the nation's annual floods has been to pass the problem on to the Fire Service and the UK Armed Forces, while encouraging local volunteers to step in. But the brutal truth is we're not properly funded to respond to or manage

---

3 Forgive me if you're picking up a bit of an edge but if there was a magic money tree, we'd be the ones called to get the cat out of it.

disasters of this kind, nor is there any statute requirement for us to do so.[4] But once the levees break and rivers start to surge, the obvious reaction is to call us in – there's simply no one else to turn to.

In many ways, we've been strong-armed into action because we want to help. As flooding has become more commonplace, Fire Services around the country have been forced into spending money on training, PPE and equipment for those types of emergencies. This money comes from other budgets earmarked for up-to-date pumps and engines or other life-saving kit. And you might think financial restraints of this kind are a new phenomenon, but they're not. When I first became a recruit in 1997, the Fire Service wasn't actually funded to attend road traffic collisions, though we trained for it and performed the task anyway. But that's what rankles most: we don't want to not get involved, it's just that we've not been charged, or assisted with the responsibility. It's as if someone in power has thought, *Well, they'll do it. They'll look bad if they don't.* And now, with the flooding problem clearly growing, the pressure on individuals like me cannot be denied.

The apparent lack of respect some sections of society have for those working in the emergency services baffles me. Politicians have cheered when doctors and nurses were denied pay rises, then expected them to stand right in the firing line of the coronavirus pandemic without the appropriate PPE. In November 2020 the TUC released

---

4 Don't believe me? Ask the union . . . 'Underfunding hit our flood response, firefighters say', FBU, 11 March 2020.

an analysis of what they called a 'decade of lost pay' for four major groups of public sector workers – teachers, refuse collectors, carers and firefighters – calculating that they were all worse off in real terms compared to 2010. In fact, firefighters saw the biggest loss of all compared to a decade previously.[5] I'm not asking you to get your violins out. After the kicking 2020 and 2021 gave us all, I don't know anyone who hasn't had to make financial sacrifices.

So, just indulge me for a while as I get this off my chest. Though what I'm about to say doesn't just concern myself. It's for colleagues in the Service too and every other hero that's had to pull on their body armour – fire-gear, or a surgical gown and face mask – in order to do their job. *Because is it OK that certain people who work for the NHS, Fire Service or Police Force can be so hard-up that using a food bank is a normal occurrence?* As far as I'm concerned, no one should have to use one, especially when there's so much wealth sloshing around the country. The sad reality is that I've heard of loads of people from the emergency services being forced into debt. They can't afford the rent to live in the communities they serve. Buying adequate food supplies for the month is sometimes an insurmountable struggle. To my mind, certain people in positions of power should be unable to sleep in their beds at night when they govern a country where millions of people are forced to rely on food banks. But perhaps that's because when I see a fire raging out of control, my instinct is to put it out.

---

5 'Public sector key workers paid over £1000 less today than a decade ago', TUC, 29 November 2020.

No one in life should suffer, but it feels extra unfair on those individuals who put their life on the line in the service of others. These days, we are expected to work until the age of sixty. I'm sure some of you might be thinking, *Oh, poor you.* Fair enough. However, let me frame it this way: a firefighter lucky enough to make it to the retirement age of sixty can expect to be physically ravaged (emotionally and mentally, they may not be in great shape either). By this point in their career, they will have spent some forty-odd years climbing ladders and crawling around on their hands and knees. Their backs and joints may have been damaged as a consequence. And all because of the physical exertions required of them in the line of duty.

The British military won't recruit soldiers in their thirties, forties or fifties because physically, most people of that age are a little off the pace. Their muscular strength declines with the passing years, as does their injury recovery rate. And yet the UK government, with their hare-brained Fire Service pension plans, would expect a much-older firefighter to climb who knows how many flights of steps in order to reach a top-floor flat at a building such as Grenfell Tower. It's a bloody joke! But that's just my personal opinion.

But anyone still in doubt as to the importance of a sensible Fire Service's retirement age should picture the following scenario:

You're trapped in a burning building, many floors up. Who do you want to see on the ground below? A watch of younger and physically fitter firefighters? Or a bunch of older ones with bad backs and dodgy knees? My dad has often said that no one wants a fire engine arriving where one of the officers' knees

goes, the other one can't find his glasses and the crew in the
back have to nip off as they're desperate for the toilet.

This is a job that makes massive demands of you.
I've watched what happens to a firefighter when they
leave the job for good at the ripe old age of fifty-five.
Without that sense of purpose and routine, they can find
it really difficult. Despite the sadness that can accompany
the departure of a good mate and colleague – or relief,
if he or she was a monumental pain in the backside – a
retirement is always celebrated with respect. It's common
to hear someone refer to the pay packets left in their last
year ('Only twelve pay packets to go . . .'). Once the final
month has passed, a close friend or two of the departing
firefighter will organise a retirement do, which always
reflects their worth in the job. At these events, there's
the guarantee that a hilarious speech will take place, there
might be a piss-taking story or two. Parties of this kind
often kick off in a function room at the local boozer
or, on some occasions, a converted fire appliance bay at
a station. I've staggered out of too many leaving dos to
remember, after rolling around with laughter.

Those final weeks can be an emotional experience for
a departing officer.[6] I've watched from the sidelines as
a variety of rituals and traditions have been laid down
on the retiree-in-waiting. At the end of their final shift,
it's standard for the oncoming and off-going watches to
dress up in their full, smart dress uniform and caps before
parading beside the fire appliances in the station. The

---

6 I've yet to go through the event myself – I still have a good few years
 to go before I start counting down my pay packets.

officer-in-charge will bring everyone to attention and deliver a brief, but always poignant, speech. Predictably, there'll be some verbal dissent in the parade of fire-fighters. Someone will often shout something out, like, 'We won't miss your farts!' or something similar.

The Fire Brigade would like to thank you for your service. We wish you a long and wonderful retirement. Be happy, stay healthy, and don't be a stranger.

There's some tat to be dished out: the departing indi-vidual will receive a letter of thanks from the Chief Fire Officer for their committed work. They'll also be given a framed Certificate of Service, a tie, some cufflinks, a tankard and all sorts of crap that will eventually make it to the back of a cupboard and never see the light of day. But there are some more heartfelt presents, too. The watch will present them with a mounted chrome-polished axe as a parting memento with all the medals they've accrued throughout their career fixed on it too. All of the firefighters I have seen retire are also presented with a brass replica BA tally. Engraved on it will be their name, service number, first day of service and last. A Breathing Apparatus tally is something that is unplugged from a firefighters BA set prior to entering a burning property. It is placed into a board, which we mount outside the property. The tally displays the firefighter's name, station, their time of entering the building and their starting air cylinder contents. It's our way of knowing who's still in a building, especially if the incident goes south.

But sometimes, if a firefighter has endured a traumatic experience, or suffered a physical or mental injury, such as PTSD, they won't want a leaving do. They'll decline the traditional gifts and routines that accompany retirement. And that's sad, but understandable. What follows for everybody, injured or healthy, can either be a transformative or destructive process.

A number of firefighters will push on from the job and find new purpose; many join the Retired Members' Association, an exclusive club that links former firefighters together and arranges a number of social events throughout the year. Essentially, it's a chance for the old gits to get together, get smashed and take the piss out of each other once more. But it's also a good way to stay mentally healthy. Too many men and women wither and fade away having left a career that meant so much to them; they lose their purpose and with it the sense of identity that defined them for so long. As I've mentioned once or twice already, the watches at each and every station function like families. There are people you love, people you love a little less, others you look up to and those that annoy the crap out of you. But giving them up is hard.

A lot of retired firefighters struggle to adjust to the realities of a life away from the mess. The chilling truth is that a high number of them don't live long into retirement. A number of them, understandably, die of cancers and other medical complaints as a result of working in an environment often scorched with carcinogens, toxins and mutagens. The number of people who get only one or two years into their retirement and pass away is tragically high – the stats would make the hair on your neck stand up. Physical ailments are only one part of the problem, though. Psychologically, it's tough too – though your body might thank you, mentally, sixty is no age to retire! Many people want to carry on working afterwards in order to keep busy, but because they've been institutionalised for so long, few of their skills are transferable to another vocation so they struggle to find work. And with nothing to mentally strive for, their body soon follows suit. Every eventual passing is a reminder of the heavy toll this job can take.[7]

That's it. Rant over, I promise. The one hope I have is that, having seen the bravery and sacrifice of the emergency services and stood on our doorsteps and clapped in celebration of the very best of humanity on the frontline during the pandemic, you take a moment when it's next time to vote to think about whether you truly believe the party you're voting for sees it as their duty to properly fund the people who pick us all up when we fall down. Anything else just isn't good enough.

---

7 And I hope you'll forgive me a moment again to reflect on a world in which firefighters are denied a fair pay rise but there was £1 trillion to bail out the banks after the 2008 crash. Come back to me with a banker who won an award for heroism in the service of banking.

16

Not All Superheroes Wear Capes (But They Do Wear PPE)

I once heard someone talking about what it means to be a firefighter and I've never forgotten it.

'There's an expectation that a firefighter will just get on with life after a horrible shout,' they said. 'People assume that you can simply absorb the trauma, no problem. No one predicts that the bad memories and negative emotions will overwhelm you, or that you might get to a point where enough is enough, and the idea hits that you've finally reached the end point and can't go any further. You think, "That's it, I need to end this noise in my head." But that's what happens sometimes because while firefighters are superheroes, they're not superhuman.'

As the words impacted on everyone in the room, we looked at each other and all seemed to think the same thing:

Fucking hell! They're right.

Immediately, I was reminded of a picture I'd once seen – a pastiche of that famous old black and white photo from the New York City skyline where a bunch of construction workers are eating their lunch on a steel girder positioned a hundred storeys up, their legs dangling off the edge. But in this updated picture, the labourers had been replaced with cartoon good guys – Spider-Man, Superman, Batman and Robin, and Thor. In the middle of the group sat a firefighter dressed in PPE. He was casually tucking into his sandwich and the others were staring at him in awe. *What's he doing here?* A firefighter can't fly like Clark Kent's alter ego. They don't possess the ability to crawl across walls like the friendly neighbourhood Spider-Man. Nor do they wield an enchanted hammer, or possess an armoury of gadgets to get them out of trouble. One slip-up here and the firefighter's dead – that PPE definitely won't save them when their arse meets the concrete.

But firefighters don't want to be superheroes. We'd much prefer it if no one crashed their car or set their house ablaze.[1] We want the people in our communities to be safe. There's also no way to technically define the act of heroism in our job because just about every shout involving fire has the potential to cause serious injury, or death. Of course, some events are objectively riskier than others. The firefighters on the scene at Grenfell Tower, the World Trade Center or even Chernobyl would have felt more in danger than the person putting out a minor bin fire somewhere else. Though I doubt any of those firefighters would ultimately have traded places for something more benign, not when there were that number of lives to be saved. Well, maybe Chernobyl.

Having said that, the person putting out a bin fire can be considered heroic too, mainly because the potential

---

[1] Or got a metal ring stuck where it doesn't belong.

for a life-changing injury is often unknown. What else has been packed inside the rubbish? In some countries, during certain moments in history, it wouldn't have been inconceivable that the fire was a trap and that an incendiary device was set to explode inside. Maybe the small blaze was bait for some violent attack – that's been known to happen too. Because of those unseen dangers, every act is one of heroism for the Fire Service. That's why people in my line of work tend to feel surprised when there's formal recognition for their efforts. As far as we're concerned, it's our job. The reward is saving lives and making a difference within our community.

There are varying styles of bravery to consider, however. Some of it is physical, plenty of it is psychological and at times it can take every ounce of strength to face a situation that ultimately might prove emotionally destructive.

Other times, I've gone above and beyond what I've been trained to do in order to save someone's life. One winter, I was part of a crew of five mobilised to a house fire. It had been a busy night; the station was stretched to the limit and there was no one else in the area to back us up immediately. Having reached the scene, it became apparent that a mother and her daughter had escaped the building, but a man was still trapped inside. The BA team rapidly deployed into the property to locate and extract him. Eventually, they pulled his body from the house and laid him on the cold wintry footpath. Myself and a colleague lifted him up and onto the rear floor of the fire engine, but the prognosis wasn't great. The bloke appeared to be dead – he wasn't breathing and there was no pulse. Our BA team then ran back into the building to bring the flames under control; the officer-in-charge was relaying a series of messages requesting back-up, and I was left with a man who seemed to have passed. I raised my line of sight and outside of the fire engine were his wife and daughter, holding one another and crying.

Bloody hell, mate, I thought. *You're going to have to get among it here.*

The Ambulance services were en route, but I knew that the only way to save his life, if it hadn't been lost already, was to apply cardiopulmonary resuscitation, or CPR, a life-saving technique in which chest compressions are applied and twinned with mouth-to-mouth breathing. (According to statistics, immediately applying CPR following a cardiac arrest can increase the chances of survival by two or three times.) But when I peered down, the task didn't seem very appealing. In those days, we weren't provided with a protective mouth shield to prevent the exchange of saliva or vomit, but the poor bloke was out cold, covered in soot and who knows what else. He was also foaming heavily at the mouth. *Ugh!* Then I looked over: his wife and daughter were staring at me.

Oh well, what else can I do? I thought.

I wiped away the foam and gloop from the victim's face best I could, tilted his head back and started mouth-to-mouth. It tasted and smelled disgusting. At first, my life-saving breaths and chest compressions didn't seem to be working, and his vital signs were non-existent. All sorts of thoughts raced through my mind in a strange stream of consciousness, one of which was the serious concern for my long-term personal health. But I carried on regardless.

This could be bad. I might catch Hepatitis C from this bloke if I'm unlucky and he's got it . . . You can't cure that, can you? Mate, I think you can die from it . . .

I paused for another breath.

Oh Jesus, his wife and kid are still staring at me! But what else am I going to do? Give up on the bloke? What did they tell us in training? 'Risk your life to save savable life in a calculated manner.' I suppose this is the very definition of that . . .

Eventually there was jerky movement and a splutter below me. My train of thought came to a screeching halt. When I looked down, the bloke was coughing and heaving. Miraculously, my efforts had saved him.

Blow me, you've done it!

An ambulance was soon on the scene and the victim and his family were whisked away to the nearest A&E department, where they were treated for various burns, bumps and bruises, and smoke inhalation. Months later, it was announced that I'd be receiving a Chief Officer's Commendation for my efforts – an award for bravery and an acknowledgement of actions above and beyond the call of duty (delivering mouth-to-mouth resuscitation without a protective shield would have done it).

The award was a shock – I was only doing my job – and it was presented to me on what turned out to be a great day out for the family, so I wasn't going to turn it down. A number of other first responders and members of the public were also receiving recognition for their work and I was eventually handed my reward – a crystal obelisk that looked as if it had arrived from the Rotary Club.

Despite the surprise, I still felt very proud, even though there was someone to pour cold water on my achievements. I remember a couple of paramedics getting quite sniffy about my being recognised for administering CPR. I suppose that's fair enough – it's something they probably had to do several times a week.

'That's part of your job!' laughed one. 'It's what you're paid for.'

He was absolutely right, but I wasn't going to let his sniping ruin my party.

'I'm not going to turn it down, am I?' I said. 'Besides, it's going to look bloody brilliant on my mantelpiece!'

Really, I couldn't have cared less about the award. What seemed more important was the fact I'd made a massive difference to that one family's life. There was the right number of faces around the dinner table that week. Without my efforts, there might have been an empty chair.

I'm not unique in overlooking risk. When it comes to fires, big and small, a firefighter will always put their life on the line for the wellbeing and survival of others, even if it means seriously injuring themselves in the process. Sometimes, though, events take place when quitting, or abandoning the effort would seem understandable to anyone watching. But that only inspires a firefighter to work even harder. Usually these are moments of such dramatic magnitude that any sense of national or international hope would crumble if the emergency services suddenly joined with the public in fleeing the scene. Terrorist attacks or natural disasters such as earthquakes fall into this category. The Australian and Californian wildfires would fit the bill entirely too.

Events of this kind inspire people to step up. Many of the men and women working through the Australia disaster of 2020 were volunteers. Of course, some of the fire crews were paid servicemen and women, but a large number risked their lives for free. I know this because around forty of their number were retired members of the British Fire Services, though a lot of red tape had to be cut in order for them to be allowed to fly over and assist with the recovery relief work. Fair play to them all. They had seen the tragedy unfolding on the news and decided to make a difference. Not one of them was rewarded financially (though some airlines covered the cost of their travel). All the volunteering men and women had begged, acquired and stolen equipment so they could work safely and effectively (well, they probably hadn't *stolen*). Thanks to their assistance, a number of communities were able to begin the long road to recovery.

The news footage and photographs that eventually filtered back from Australia during that time were terrifying, almost apocalyptic. A world of ash and smoke and death. Herds of animals. I remember thinking, *Thank God, we don't have* that *here.* And while the Australian Fire Services had the tools and techniques to deal with incidents of that nature, they were at times overwhelmed. There were scenes of traffic jams miles long as thousands of families tried to escape the devastation, their homes and lives in ashes, all of them heading in one direction.

On the other side of the road, speeding towards the intimidating flames was a convoy of fire trucks. The firefighters in those vehicles understood that they represented the last line of defence in a battle between fire and a series of vulnerable communities and ecosystems. The sight of kangaroos and koalas, singed by the extreme heat and clearly distressed, being pulled to safety was incredibly moving. At the same time, the knowledge that every firefighter involved was giving everything to halt the destruction filled me with pride.

All of them were superheroes in PPE, but none of them would have expected a crystal obelisk for their efforts.

The people I work with aren't even that fussed about getting a thank you from those we save, though, for the most part, the public can be pretty grateful when it comes to the work of the emergency services. Some of them are even apologetic. One time, my station was called to a flooding incident when a pipe had ruptured in an upstairs flat within a small apartment block. A little old lady had called us: apparently, water was rushing down her walls.

'I'm terribly sorry to have called you,' she said, once the problem had been fixed. 'I know you're so busy and you do such a wonderful job, but once my light fitting started sparking, I thought it'd be prudent to call for help.'

Even animals can appear grateful following a shout, but you won't be surprised to learn that the beasts in question have always been dogs rather than cats.[2] As an animal lover myself, I'll happily run into a burning building to rescue the family pet, though I always advise untrained members of the public against doing the same, especially after having once attended a fire in a flat when a woman, pinned to her balcony by flames, dashed back inside to

---

2 And I've always found hamsters to be indifferent.

retrieve her dog. The people talking to her below had begged her not to go in, but there was no persuading her. By the time we'd arrived on the scene, she hadn't been seen for a couple of minutes.

The door was breached and as part of the BA team, we worked our way through the flat, the fire still raging around us. It was hot, too hot to stand up. Our search had to be done on our hands and knees. Using a thermal imaging camera, I scanned the rooms for the woman. I eventually found her, lying face down on the floor in her lounge, unconscious. Dead? We didn't know! We quickly scooped her up and made our way back out of the inferno, handing her over to colleagues, who were waiting outside to administer emergency resuscitation. Then we swiftly made our way back into the flat. My colleague started to manage the flames with our hose-reel, while I scanned the room for her dog. Bingo (that wasn't its name), I found it. *It was fucking huge!* A large Alsatian, it didn't seem to be faring so well. It was lifeless, lying behind the telly, where it must have been shielding from the heat. I picked it up and we withdrew, leaving the fire with a second BA team that had been committed. I laid the dog on the grass outside and as far as I was concerned, it hadn't made it. Then I returned to the flat to help the others.

When the blaze was finally extinguished, we exited the building.

'Where's the dead dog?' I asked one of my colleagues – it wasn't where I'd left it.

The firefighter pointed: 'What, *that* dead dog?'

There was the Alsatian. It was jumping between all the firefighters, licking hands and gobbling down biscuits.

I couldn't believe it. The mutt had been out cold only minutes earlier; I'd presumed it was on its way to the great kennel in the sky. When it saw me, the dog went berserk. It bounded over at full speed and wrapped itself around my legs, tail wagging frantically. The dog seemed to sense I'd been the one that had carried it to safety, even though it was unconscious at the time.

Sometimes, acts of gratitude can arrive from nowhere, when simply being a firefighter can get you places – and in style, too. Twenty years back myself, Dad and a close colleague flew to New York – we'd gone after I struck up a friendship with a firefighter from the Engine 54 Ladder 4 Company on Eighth Avenue. Previously, I'd travelled to Manhattan in 1998 and on a whim popped into the first fire station I passed – I wanted to say hello and get a feel for how the job was done across the pond. Once welcomed inside, I met a bloke called Lenny Regaglia and we hit it off straight away, staying in contact through email for a few years until I received some tragic news in the days following the 9/11 attacks: Lenny had been killed when the Twin Towers collapsed. I felt devastated. On top of so much horror, the realisation that the firefighter I'd known had been lost in the tragedy brought everything so much closer to home.

Out of respect for the friendship we'd formed, the Engine & Ladder Company invited me to his funeral. It was to take place on Staten Island, just across the water from the very scene of the attacks. At that time, there was an admiration for firefighters the world over.

The efforts of the emergency services in New York had drawn global praise and as the three of us settled into our economy seats, hanging up our ceremonial uniforms in a cupboard at the front of the cabin, a stewardess came over for some small talk.

'Where are you three going then?' she said gesturing to the suits. 'I noticed your bags . . . A wedding?'

I told her the story about Lenny, our friendship and what had happened.

'I'm so very sorry,' said the stewardess. 'Don't say anything, grab your stuff and come with me.'

Dad looked over at me fretfully: 'What's going on here?'

'Gentlemen, you're moving seats,' whispered the stewardess. 'There's no way three members of the Fire Service should be sitting here! I'd like you to enjoy Business Class seats on us.'

I couldn't believe it. For seven hours, we were able to live the jet-set lifestyle. Unbelievably, we even got the same treatment on the way back as it was the same aircrew.

Some of the words I mentioned earlier need a little contextualisation at this point: *a respect for firefighters the world over.* Like paramedics, the police, or anyone working in service of their community – where horrific accidents, or injury, are a very real and present danger – the idea of respect is not a universal concept. There have been some instances when firefighters from another Brigade have been assaulted during riots, as double-decker buses and police vehicles were destroyed, and homes and businesses smashed up and set ablaze. At which point the Fire

Service were called in to control the fires.

Beautiful old buildings were going up in flames. Because of their age, the structures alongside them were catching fire too and the enormity of the job seemed daunting to anyone working on the ground. As a viewer to the situation, at home, watching on the telly, the task seemed ridiculous. What made matters worse was the hostile vibe around the place.

The riot police were bombarded with bricks and petrol bombs. Ambulances in attendance were treated just as badly. And every time a fire engine arrived on the scene, they were attacked too. Yet every single individual working on the ground still pressed ahead with the job, determined to protect the community they served. Some of them later went to hospital for their efforts, their injuries caused by malice rather than misfortune. I couldn't believe what I'd seen once the violence had calmed down, days later.

Political anger and protest I could understand, but a show of aggression towards the very people putting their life on the line for the greater good of the community seemed like stupidity on a whole other level and, sadly, it's not uncommon. The chilling statistic is that in England in 2016, around 200 firefighters were attacked by people we'll politely call 'wallies'. A few years later, in 2018–19, that number rose to 961; 1,170 including Wales, Northern Ireland and Scotland. I am a public servant and so are my watch mates; I understand my responsibilities and accept all the risks and occupational hazards attached. *We all do.* But with one exception: Please, *please*, please don't chuck bricks and bottles at us when we're trying to contain an inferno on your doorstep.

We do our job well, we don't expect a show of gratitude. The community contributes its taxes, so everyone within it is entitled to our help, should trouble arise – and we're more than happy to provide that service, regardless of some of the unpleasantness that can take place. I've resuscitated people on the street and crawled on my hands and knees through buildings on fire to drag people to safety. I've spent hours inside the twisted wreckage of car crashes, reassuring the injured passengers that they're going to make it out alive. I've climbed into trees to coax a family cat to the ground and been bitten by a Jack Russell. I've seen all manner of horrors, but I've also witnessed the relief among a family as they've been rescued from a burning building in one piece. That, for me, is enough – in fact, it's a privilege.

I don't need thanks, I don't need medals. And I certainly don't need a million quid in the bank (though I wouldn't grumble at a pay rise in line with inflation every year). I just want to help. But there are some things I've seen that I'll never get over.

17

After the Fire

A number of years ago, I was among the first officers in attendance at an event I still find it difficult to think about now. I'm not able to talk about it in detail but it involved an incident with a number of bodies and it rocked me like nothing ever had before. The smell was overpowering, too. At a fire incident, the sweet stench of burnt flesh will never stop being disturbing. Any kind of dead body carries a pungent whiff and it's an aroma that will never, ever leave you. It seems to cling to the nostrils for weeks and months on end and as a cordon was being set up around this incident, the pong of death suffocating me, I started to feel quite overwhelmed.

As one of the incident commanders at the scene, it was my responsibility to protect the wellbeing of the other men and women of the Fire Service. I knew there was an enormous risk to their psychological safety and I needed to protect them. I decided to make a precautionary radio call.

'I do not want any Fire Service personnel coming into the police cordon area,' I said. 'It's unnecessary. There's nothing that can be done by us here.'

Just by standing in the cordoned-off area and communicating with members of the police and ambulance services, I felt as if I was absorbing wave after wave of trauma. *Drip, drip, drip.* By the time I'd left work for home, I was in a heady state of shock. I couldn't comprehend what I'd just experienced. And then the story got picked up by the media. For the rest of the day, I moved through a waking nightmare, the high-definition images in my head tearing down my resilience minute after minute.

I'd spoken to many firefighters who attended Grenfell in the aftermath of that terrible tragedy. Their experiences from that night made for harrowing listening and while they were undeniably scarred by what had taken place, the fact that the story then consumed the nation for weeks on end only amplified their emotional suffering too. Many of them had lived in the neighbourhood. The tower stood as a blackened tomb within the community they'd served. Journalists were camped outside Latimer Road tube station and the Westway football pitches nearby. Flowers were pinned to railings on the street. Members of the Royal Family had attended the scene and Prime Minister Theresa May famously angered the local residents by apparently not talking to them during her visit. Every incident generated a headline; every headline left an emotional scar for those individuals who had to run up and down the staircase of Grenfell Tower. I'm sure the surviving firefighters in attendance at 9/11, the 7/7 tube bombings, or the London Bridge terrorist attacks would have experienced something similar. Once an event like this hits the breaking news cycle, it can become all-consuming.

I can't lie, being a firefighter has taken its toll. Not just on my back and knees, but on my emotions, too. When I first started the job as a green twenty-one-year-old, very little was done to mentally and emotionally prepare me for what I was about to see, hear and even smell in the line of duty. Yeah, I'd met with Doctor Death and his Portfolio of Blood, but his lessons were a relatively one-dimensional introduction to what a burns victim might look like, or what I could expect to witness during a road traffic collision shout. These days, the process is much more considered and controlled. New recruits, as I've mentioned previously, are gently eased into the more traumatic aspects of the job. But for my generation, the exposure to trauma felt quicker, more extreme. As a result, my mental wellbeing has taken a beating, as it would for anyone where gore and tragedy can appear regularly and at any time.

In the early days of the job, shortly after completing the RTC (road traffic collision) phase of training, I remember feeling a sense of anticipation about witnessing my first death. It wasn't something I was excited about – I certainly don't want anybody thinking I was eager for someone to die. Rather, I needed to know whether I had the stomach for it. That first car smash made me think that I could cope (though I'd argue I was in a state of denial at the time, especially when I told friends the incident hadn't affected me that much). What I hadn't realised was that emotional trauma often affected a person cumulatively and I would suffer over time. In many ways, a person's capacity for coping can be compared to a coffee mug positioned under a broken tap.

Drip, drip, drip.

At first, the water gathering in the cup seems insignificant.

Drip, drip, drip.

But after a while, a series of drips fills the cup. It brims at the edges until one final drop causes it to overflow.

Drip, drip, drip.

Drip, drip, drip.

My mind suffered a similar fate.

Everybody's emotional cup is different. Some are large, some are small. Some are easily chipped, others seem incredibly resistant when dropped on the floor. That means all of us are different when it comes to absorbing stress and horror. Some firefighters I've known have been lucky. They've worked for years and years without seeing an unsettling experience, though they're very much in the minority. Others have been upended during their first traumatic shout. A small number of those people left the job as soon as they'd started – it's all a bit of a lottery.

My luck seemed to hold firm at first. The brutalities of being a firefighter seemed to land a few early glancing blows, but nothing I couldn't handle. Then I noticed some of the older hands on the watch as they struggled to absorb what was happening in front of their eyes. Their reactions were particularly acute when it came to road traffic collisions, especially if kids were involved. At the scene they would look troubled. Some of them hung back, volunteering themselves for a task away from the vehicles, or victims. Later, as the group decompressed back in the station mess, those individuals would seem visibly shaken and the watch would rally around them.

In the first flushes of my career I couldn't get my head around it.

I'd think, *What's wrong with you? This is the job. If you can't handle it, maybe this line of work isn't for you.*

Just writing that sentence down now, twenty-five years later, I'll acknowledge that my response was very naive and insensitive. But that's just the way I was back then. I'm very different now. Over the course of my career, I've realised that my actions were a self-defence mechanism and I was convincing myself that my mental health was in good nick. Certainly, I was in a very different headspace to the more senior people at the station. They had wives, husbands and long-term partners. A lot of them were parents. In terms of their careers, they were nearer to the end than the beginning. I suppose with regards to their own mortality, they had endured one or two scrapes that had made them more appreciative of life and so any unpleasantness in the job was felt more keenly. At the same time, I was young and yet to become a dad – my attitude towards risk and the human condition was a lot more casual.

This emotional position was reinforced when Dad said something to me a few years later. We had been operational firefighters together for a while by that point and the closer he'd got to his retirement, the more death and destruction seemed to affect him negatively. Life had become more precious too. One night, after a particularly rough shift, he called me up.

'If I never, ever see another dead person in a car, I'll be OK with that,' he said.

A few years on, I began to feel exactly the same way. Seeing people die started to hit me harder; suddenly I was the one having that wobble in the station mess as I absorbed the tragedies more and more. Today, it's advanced even further and it would be nice to guarantee that I'll never be called to a fatal road traffic collision ever again, though I know that's unlikely. I'm not the only one to feel that way either. I remember being on a shout where a number of stations were brought together in order to get the job done. One of the firefighters in attendance was on the verge of retirement, one pay packet left, and having learned that a particularly gruesome scene had unfolded inside the burning building, he asked to be assigned to a task away from the dead bodies that were being retrieved.

'I don't need it,' he said. 'I don't need to see it. There's nothing that can be done for those people. I've got a month to go and it's been five years since my last fatality – that one fucked me up enough. I don't need to see a new one just as I'm about to retire.'

The officer-in-charge was a good leader. He understood that unnecessarily exposing a firefighter on the verge of leaving to a harrowing experience might carry potentially life-changing implications.

'You sit there,' he said. 'You're absolutely correct, don't fuck your head up.'

It was 100 per cent the right call.

A series of horrors have struck me over my twenty-five-year career. I attended car smashes where couples, or entire families, had been pinned inside a vehicle. The injuries were stomach-churning and on more than one occasion one of the people inside died before we were able to cut them out. It would be my job to sit with the hysterical wife or husband as they screamed in emotional anguish and physical pain. During those moments, the feelings were incredibly destructive. Often I experienced a sense of shock; the idea that nothing could be done for the deceased left an awful sense of guilt and sadness at the time, and the emotional trauma experienced by the survivors created a fair amount of scars too.

Drip, drip, drip . . . My metaphorical coffee cup was beginning to fill up.

I've even seen people set themselves on fire. Like all suicide attempts, events of this kind take place because of a dangerous combination of complex emotional problems and troubling circumstances and they're always difficult to comprehend, especially when the death takes place in front of your very eyes. On this occasion, they had doused themself in petrol. As we arrived on scene they struck the match, they were immediately engulfed in flames and running around, leaving a trail of flaming footprints behind them. Rigged in my BA I went after them, and when I reached out to grab their arm, a perfectly formed sleeve of flesh came away. Several layers of skin had been roasted into a limb-shaped cast and I was left staring for the briefest of moments – I couldn't shake that sight from my eyes for years afterwards.

One or two moments have been even more impactful. During a road traffic collision, I was accidentally nicked with a used surgical needle while emergency treatment was taking place on the scene. The individual we'd been treating was a former addict and upon arrival in the emergency room, they were told what had happened to me and the concerns for my health.

Had I been infected with something terrible?

A doctor leaned over the injured man's stretcher to relay the news. He said, 'We're going to run some blood tests. Would you mind us sharing the results so this fire-fighter can decide upon a course of action?'

The individual we'd just saved shook his head.

'No.'

No.

That one word put me through three months of anxiety. I was forced to wait out the typical, three-month incubation period for HIV or Hepatitis, all the while fearing that my life was forever changed, knowing that a positive diagnosis would seriously affect my mortality.

My life got darker from there. Overnight, I became vulnerable and the stress later forced me into another period of therapy as I attempted to reconcile my anger and fears. I turned to DJ'ing to ease my stress. House music became my release and I later secured a radio residency and some great club appearances at renowned venues such as the Ministry of Sound. I also made a number of incredible friends within the industry. While that was going on, my two families – the one at home and the Fire Service – propped me up during the turbulent moments. My station commander was incredible and he would ring up at least three times a week to make sure I was OK. My Occupational Health team was an effective resource too. When I later received the all-clear, I felt as if a huge weight had been lifted from my shoulders, but my worldview was forever changed.

But in the wake of the event at the beginning of this

chapter, my day-to-day life had become a minefield. Images from the incident seemed to show up whenever I turned on the telly. Facebook and Twitter became swamped by news updates on the tragedy.

I'd started to suffer PTSD (post-traumatic stress disorder).

The condition, which affects all sorts of people, from military veterans to witnesses of a particularly violent crime, can be unpredictable. For me, different trigger points seemed to set off subconscious shockwaves. Sometimes a sound would unsettle me, other times it was a visual cue. A certain time of day might spark off a mood. Different smells and tastes could upend me too. And when these moments arrived, I was transported mentally to a series of incidents and events from my fire-fighting career. None of them were particularly pleasant and it was as if a 'greatest hits' of death and tragedy was playing through my mind on a loop.

I might walk past a kebab shop or a restaurant and notice the smell of cooking. Momentarily, I'd be thrust back to a car, turned upside down on the roadside, the passengers inside slowly dying in front of me. Or I'd flash back to an event in a burning building, where I'd dragged a corpse onto the lawn outside. The sweet, sickly aroma of what was cooking in that takeaway had created an echo of something far more unpleasant. At times, it was a struggle to get a handle on myself. Whenever I became affected, I'd try to talk myself down, or I'd attempt to steer my thinking towards something more positive and present. But rational thought seemed impossible. I'd wake with the night terrors. A nightmare had dragged me back

to a fire or a traffic incident from ten years earlier, but
in the swirl of my dreamlike state, every sight and sound
felt so much more vivid – my head was hellish at times.

The trauma was hypnotic. I could be in a park, with
my kids, watching them laughing and playing. Suddenly
I'd be transported back. In the moment, I'd almost look
down at myself in an out-of-body experience.

I was with my family, they were having a great time.

But emotionally, I was a million miles away. I can
remember fighting my way psychologically back to a
sense of reality, but every time the process was gruelling.

I'd talk myself round: 'Mate, you're in a park with your
kids. You need to get these thoughts out of your head.'

Other times, my detachment from whatever was going
on around me would become apparent to other people.
I'd be eating dinner at home, or in a restaurant, when
suddenly, from nowhere, I would hear a voice calling me
back to reality – my wife's, or a mate's. It was as if they
were trying to reach me through a fog. In an instant, life
would come rushing at me with a jarring lucidity. I'd
been emotionally drifting, staring into space.

I was back there again.

When I looked down, my hands were shaking.

I needed help.

During my early years as a firefighter, there was a very
different attitude to the issues of emotional injury and
mental health. A large number of individuals from the
older generation were still in place. And while undoubt-
edly caring people, there was a tendency to gloss over
some of the more emotionally challenging events that

their watch might have experienced. Blokes that had visibly struggled in the aftermath of a shout were told to 'go to the cupboard and get a can of man-up'. Women suffering from stress were encouraged to 'get used to it'. That was how it had been in my dad's day, as well as my grandad's and my uncle's too. When I signed up with the Fire Service, the last vestiges of that era were still in place.

It's very different today. There's a much more open and empathetic culture in place. I've been in mess rooms where the watch has gathered around someone overwhelmed by what they've seen during a shout. The mood is always supportive.

'Have a cry, mate,' someone will say. 'Get it out.'

There have been occasions when I've even instructed people to go home in the middle of a shift, having recognised that they'd probably benefit from being with their family during a tricky moment. Hanging around in a state of shock when death, or the memory of some horrific injury, lurks on the peripheries of the mind does no one any favours in the long run.

My individual nature has served me well as I've progressed into the role of a watch commander. I invest in the relationships of everyone I work with because knowing them intimately helps me to recognise when they might be harbouring emotions. As laughter is the best medicine, I encourage humour every time we're on duty and keep my watch propped up with a constant flow of top-quality Dad jokes. I understand all too well the psychological and emotional bruises that can land on someone during the job. In the hours, days and weeks after a difficult incident, I'll give them the time they need to manage their feelings. If a deeper layer of support is necessary, I will refer them to our incredible occupational health professionals.

Being screwed-up by the job can force a firefighter into a dark and lonely place sometimes. I know – I've been there myself. In those times, it was a massive comfort that the people around me would listen happily to my stresses and provide support during tough times, rather than tell me to ride it out with bravado, or eat a spoonful of cement. In that way, the job has progressed and I'm very happy about it.

This approach runs across the Service now and over the years we've all come to understand how the job can affect the people functioning within it, especially after really traumatic incidents. Over the years, certain protocols have been put in place that ensure a person can receive assistance following a difficult job and one of these is the Trauma Risk Management process (TRiM for short). Briefly . . . following a nasty event, the incident commander will gather together the names of every firefighter in attendance. That list is then forwarded to a TRiM co-ordinator, who will contact those individuals. During these contacts, they will decide if someone needs any further help, signposting them accordingly.

For example, it might be that someone has psychologically normalised a very extreme event and says they're OK when really, they're not. In the following days and weeks, they might experience unsettling emotions or reactions to everyday events. The TRiM process shows them that the strange emotions they're experiencing are very normal under the circumstances. If required, they'll signpost them to incredible Occupational Health, who in turn will arrange the appropriate support, such as Cognitive Behavioural Therapy (CBT).

As the days and weeks passed, following my exposure to the tragedy, it became very clear from my TRiM assessment that I would need additional support. The night terrors worsened, I became more and more detached and when my mental and emotional state was assessed, I was diagnosed with PTSD. But I was OK with that. Having worked with one or two mental health professionals throughout my career, I'd become fairly comfortable with the process of therapy.

Then, at the beginning of 2020, after more therapy, it was decided I should intensify the healing process with a period of Eye Movement Desensitization and Reprocessing (EMDR). I felt excited at the suggestion. Following some online research, I learned that EMDR was a relatively recent addition to the practice of psychotherapy and had been successfully used on combat veterans and other members of the emergency services. According to webmd.com:

An EMDR treatment session can last up to 90 minutes. Your therapist will move his or her fingers back and forth in front of your face and ask you to follow these hand motions with your eyes. At the same time, the EMDR therapist will have you recall a disturbing event.

This will include the emotions and body sensations that go along with it. Gradually, the therapist will guide you to shift your thoughts to more pleasant ones. Some therapists use alternatives to finger movements, such as hand or toe tapping, or musical tones.

It all sounded pretty interesting, though, honestly, I would have tried just about anything to shut down the negative emotions that kept striking at me from out of nowhere. But just as I was about to begin work on my personal recovery, March 2020 landed and with it, coronavirus and the national lockdown. Life ground to a halt, and like so many other people across the country suffering mental health issues, my treatment was put on hold. I felt devastated.

My therapist called me on Skype: 'I'm not sure what we're going to do, Leigh,' she said. 'EMDR is a face-to-face exercise only, we can't do this treatment effectively via Skype.'

Cooped up at home, my life seemed to cave in. I had my wife and kids for support, but what I really needed was professional help. And that's when I was introduced to Jacqui Wilmshurst, a risk psychologist. Jacqui had operated in Afghanistan, where she'd trained journalists working in hairy situations. She'd also worked in the Balkans with NATO and in Northern Ireland on crisis operations. These experiences had led her to develop and trademark a personal risk management tool based on psychology and neuroscience research called Managing Psychological Safety (MaPS). Her work was then signed off by a number of prestigious trauma therapy experts. As I'd come to discover, Jacqui's methods were the real deal.

When we eventually met, she laid out what her work would involve. 'This is not a reactive process, Leigh,' she explained. 'It won't erase what's come before. But what I can do is present you with a system of education, one that will give you the tools to manage a trauma *before you actually experience the trauma itself.* Nobody knows

your body better than you. If you can understand how
and why you react to certain emotions, you'll be able
to handle them a whole lot better.'

Over a number of months, while shut away in my house
like the rest of the world, I progressed through her workshops, locating the tools that would enable me to understand
my mind during times of future crisis. I learned how to
manage my feelings in times of stress and how to break
down overwhelming and heavy experiences into smaller,
more manageable problems. In the past, I'd compartmen-
talised my troubles and tried to forget about them. But
while any fears and stresses I'd experienced were out of
sight, they were still there. Nothing had been managed, not
really, and in a way, my traumas had been bottled up like
a fizzy drink. Every new negative experience caused them
to shake violently, adding to the pressure already building
inside. It was only a matter of time before the lid popped
off and my issues exploded all over the place, impacting
on my life and the lives of my friends and family, both
at home and in the job. I'd read too many horror stories
of people lashing out at their wives or kids. A number of
people in jobs like mine had even taken their own lives.
I didn't want to be another grim statistic.

With Jacqui's MaPS system, I was able to dissect my
emotions, by first acknowledging them and then locating
the reasons why they were so upsetting. From that point,
I was able to learn why I had become emotionally unbal-
anced and what I could do to rectify the situation. On
those occasions where I'd wandered past a café and a
smell had transported me back to a scene from my past,
I was able to manage the flashbacks.

I'd ask, 'But why had that smell unsettled me?'
Because the smell had clung to my nostrils for weeks.
Then, 'Why was that upsetting?'
Because it reminded me of all the death.
I'd conclude, 'But you're not there anymore, mate. That moment's gone.'
You're safe.

Breaking down those larger, unpleasant moments couldn't erase them from my memory entirely; from time to time, I'll still vividly remember what I've seen but I now experience those moments from a position of perspective. I can recall and observe the events, rather than reliving them, because Jacqui's workshops have helped me get a handle on how I can manage the traumatic emotions from my life. I have plenty of dark materials in the corners of my head. Being a firefighter is an emotionally turbulent job and I've absorbed plenty of stuff that I wish I hadn't. As a result, my mind can feel like a right mess at times. Luckily, I'm in a position to work with my issues and find the solutions for myself.

I have PTSD – you might have noticed I'm not ashamed to admit it. *But why would I be?* Thanks to Jacqui, plus a network of good people around me and the Fire Service, I'm able to fight my demons more effectively. Today, I have the weapons required to win what has been a succession of psychological wars.

Hopefully, that large traumatic incident was the last one I'll ever have to face, but what I also know is I won't be able to pick and choose the firecalls I attend. Every day, I live with the knowledge that the next shout might be the one I don't get over.

Epilogue:
Everyday Heroes

Picture any fire station. Some firefighters chatting in the mess, some training in the gym together, some studying for exams. If they haven't already, every single one of them will experience the highs and lows I've described. I have had countless conversations with people who don't work in the Fire Service and find it hard to understand how we do our job.

At the beginning of my book, I told you I had the best job in the world – allow me to explain why.

Firefighters are a unique breed. It takes a certain kind of individual to enter a burning building to rescue someone they have never met before. It takes a particular type of character to comfort those who have lost everything they have ever known. You are completely reliant upon the highly trained team around you, made up of every sort of person present in the communities it serves and protects.

Firefighters are inspirational. They empower each other to get the job done and their trust and faith in their collective ability gives them the confidence to be dauntless at every incident they attend.

These men and women of our fire and rescue services have a strength of character that goes beyond words. They are the best kind of human beings imaginable: caring, considerate, resilient, empathetic, honest, adaptable, trustworthy, dedicated, courageous, and selfless. They are also some of the funniest people you could ever meet.

Firefighters are a family away from family. In every fire station around the world you find circles of intimate trust, laughter and the sort of mutual banter you find in families. The trauma and emotional pain experienced in the discharge of their duty can leave its mark, scars that stay with us. Some are more resilient than others and some find it too hard to carry on. Humour and light-heartedness are an essential coping mechanism for firefighters, a vital pressure release. Laughter allows light into dark spaces.

I have had times when I have felt like I can't do the job anymore, but I have found the fortitude to carry on, because someone needs to be there.

There will always be that dropped cigarette, that distracting phone call on a wet motorway. People will always need someone to stride towards the danger. And I am proud that I do that with the men and women who make up our Fire Service.

To continually witness bravery and dedication is a privilege. I have seen terrible things but my firefighting family has been there for me, as I have for them, and brought me back from dark places to laugh harder than

I have ever laughed before. And I have drunk more cups of salty tea than you've had hot dinners.

The station lights flash on and the mobilisation alarm sounds! Coffee mugs hit the table, chairs scrape back, we're off again. The best job in the world!

This book could save your life

#1 You have no excuses for not buying that bloody smoke alarm – *right away*.

Yes, they can be annoying. OK, they go off at the slightest whiff of burning toast and yes, the low battery alert is a pain in the arse, too. I know, I know, *I know*! However, the chilling reality is that most fire-related deaths occur in homes that haven't got a working alarm. When a blaze begins, a house can very quickly become choked with smoke. This has the potential to kill everyone sleeping inside, so for the sake of around seven quid, there's really no reason not to have one set up. And if you can't afford it, your local Fire Service should be able to offer you free alarms and installation.

#2 Formulate an exit strategy.

Plan an emergency escape strategy for your home. Where are your door keys? (Somewhere accessible, please.) Which room will you retreat to in the event of your exit being blocked by fire? (Clue: the one nearest the street so you can be rescued easily.) Who's getting the kids and who's phoning the Fire Service? These decisions are individual and unique to you, your family and your home. But start planning your strategy today. As people have said during the outbreaks of pandemics, precautionary action always feels over the top until, suddenly, the moment arrives when it doesn't – take the same attitude towards fire.

#3 Take care behind the wheel.

In a modern society, where we all have moral obligations (unless you're a senior advisor to the Prime Minister, that is), taking care when driving tonnes of steel, rubber and highly flammable fuel at speed should be a given. Except it isn't. In 2017, it was reported that 33 people died at the wheel while using their mobile phones. In 2018, it was estimated that 240 deaths on the road happened as a result of drink driving. And in 2019, there were a total of 1,752 deaths on the UK's roads. So here are some rules to live by:

1) Don't drink beyond the legal limit, or get high or stoned, and then drive home. Your reactions are greatly reduced, which increases your risk of having an accident.

2) Use a Bluetooth hands-free phone device for when you're behind the wheel. Even better, save the communications until you're home. Texting, swiping on Tinder, or ranting at Piers Morgan on social media is a death wish when driving.

3) Remember those gory adverts from a few years back and wear a seat belt in both the front and back of a vehicle – it can save your life and the lives of those around you.

4) Look after your emergency services worker. My

mental health, and the mental health of so many other firefighters, police officers and paramedics, will be all the better for not having to scrape your remains off the inside of a vehicle.

#4 Tailing a fire engine on a blue light is not smart.

When answering emergency calls, firefighters are authorised to break certain speed limits and pass through red traffic lights with caution – but only if it's safe to do so. Those rules don't apply to anyone else, and anyone following a fire engine that's breaking the speed limit, or driving through a red light, is open to prosecution. It's bloody dangerous too. By hanging in the slipstream of a fast-moving emergency vehicle, a motorist can endanger the lives of everyone on the road nearby. At the same time, firefighters have to 'drive to arrive' and it takes an incredible amount of skill and concentration to do so successfully. If an appliance driver is being distracted in their side-view mirrors by a closely following car, the chances of them getting to a destination safely are drastically reduced.

#5 Think before you dial 999.

Your stranded cat, caught halfway up an oak tree, is not a 999 event. A broken aerial on the roof is not a 999 event either. Nor is being locked out of your house on a freezing-cold day (caveat: unless you genuinely have a roast dinner in the oven and it's on the verge of going up in flames, or you are old and frail). You might think I'm being a little overzealous, but the Fire Brigade is constantly being asked to solve these issues. These calls are a complete waste of everyone's time. Instead, go online, find a contractor and pay for the work to be completed. (We were also once asked to free an old chap who claimed to have been trapped in his Spitfire cockpit, but it turned out the poor old war veteran had dementia and was locked in his flat. On that occasion, we were more than happy to help.)

#6 Fire hydrants and their parking spots are for fire engines.

If you're one of the many people that have been selfish or silly enough to park over a bright yellow fire hydrant, I have zero sympathy for you when your car is nudged out of the way by a fire engine. Or broken into and moved. Or bumped to one side. A special place in hell has been reserved for those individuals who believe the walking distance from their front door to their steering wheel supersedes the necessary life-saving resources at the fingertips of the Fire Service.

#7 DIY is dangerous . . .

So do your homework. I'm not saying you *shouldn't* spend your bank holiday weekend in Wickes when you could be hanging out with your loved ones. What I *am* saying is that some DIY equipment, not used carefully, is a 999 call waiting to happen. As are the kickbacks from poorly considered projects, such as the construction of a brick pizza oven next to a heavily creosoted fence (homemade pepperoni specials won't taste so good once the garden's ablaze). And never set fire to an old shed. Do the right thing: dismantle it properly and take it to the rubbish dump like a sensible member of society.

#8 Candles: beware.

I like a scented candle as much as the next metro-sexual male, but there's no way I'd let anyone in my family position them all over my house, especially with the kids running around. One accident and it's goodbye, carpets; goodbye, curtains; goodbye, soft furnishings. No one wants the family home to be transformed into a pyrotechnics show. The same goes for cheap Christmas decorations too. Dry pine trees + highly flammable plastic + naked flames = a miserable festive season on a par with the *EastEnders* Christmas special.

#9 Remember, remember the 5th of November . . .

And stay indoors, close the curtains and pretend it's not happening. I'm joking. Fireworks look like a lot of fun, they sound like a lot of fun, they are a lot of fun. Sadly though, a large number of responsible adults in the UK tend not to run through the type of health and safety checks required for the most modest of garden displays. Rockets are accidentally launched into a neighbour's garden. Catherine wheels go rogue. Sparklers are transformed into miniature IEDs. I should know: my firefighting dad was a serial offender when it came to Bonfire Night and very nearly became the scourge of the neighbourhood. My advice: go to a professionally organised display. You'll enjoy it more, save a load of cash and reduce the odds of losing an eye.

#10 Protect your local fire station.

As the UK government looks to cut public service expenditure further, the axe may fall on your local fire station to enable them to make these cuts. Fire authorities are required to consult with the public, so have your say, use your voice and save your local Fire Service.

Because cuts cost lives!

And finally . . .

#11 Never put a bit of yourself into anything you wouldn't be happy for me (and several of my colleagues) to come and remove with our terrifying-looking equipment.

Acknowledgements

Mark Twain once said 'to get the full value of joy you must have somebody to divide it with.' This book has been a labour of love. An emotional rollercoaster to write – hilarious, heartwarming and heartbreaking. But it wouldn't have been possible on my own.

To Jamie Coleman, my editor. Thank you for the opportunity for me to share my story. Your editorial guidance along the way has been invaluable. Thank you also to everyone at Orion and Trapeze. You have made me feel incredibly valued.

To my agent Rory Scarfe and The Blair Partnership. Your professionalism, support and industry knowledge has given me such an amazing experience; one that I will cherish forever. I have learned so much from you all. You are second to none at what you do and I can't thank you enough.

To Matt Allen, my literary alchemist and range finder. There aren't enough words to express my gratitude, mate. Your skill and talent have been an absolute pleasure to work with. To the moon. . .

To my close colleagues, extended fire family, friends

and confidants, thank you. Especially: Dave, Alan, Steve, Zach, Scott, Nikki, Dany, Ricky, Mo, Westley, Anna, Simon G, Moses, John R and Russell B. There were times when I wasn't sure if my balance of humour and honesty were proportionate, and there were times when I was unboxing a lot of darkness, things that had laid dormant in my mind for many years. Your advice, inspiration, humour and friendship along the way gave me courage, strength and a bearing when I needed it the most. I'm indebted to you all.

To my hilarious lefty comrades: Brian, Ian, Steve, Mark and Karl. Thank you for some of the funniest fire brigade stories and humour I have ever heard.

To my laugh-out-loud friend Vanessa Marcie: continue to lead with humour.

Thanks Jacqui Wilmshurst. You are a lifesaver!

To my beautiful family: to say I've been a little preoccupied would be an understatement. To my beautiful caring mum, thank you for all you do and all you are. To my children, Eevee, Enzo and Sienna. And to my sister, Michael, Daisy, Harriette. Your love, understanding, help and flexibility over the past three years has given me the space to achieve my goal. Thank you all.

Ma belle chérie. You are the rock I needed on this journey. The constant foundation for our family and my writing. You kept the cogs turning at home and maintained a sense of normality for everyone whilst I was absent in my endeavour. If this wasn't enough on its own, you gave up much of your own downtime to read and re-read my manuscript, making sure it was the best it could be. I can't thank you enough for your belief in me, your critique and encouragement. You're the best – Je t'aime xxx

Uncle Colin: your wise words and shared life experience has been influential. Keep smiling!

Grandad Ron & Uncle Trevor – Rest in Peace. One hand for yourselves, one hand for the job.

Dad: my incredible father, my friend, my colleague, my inspiration. Being able to follow in your footsteps was a dream come true, and to this day is still an absolute honour and privilege. I still pinch myself from time to time as I can't believe I get to do what I do for a living. I owe you an eternal debt of gratitude for the encouragement and support you gave me so I could become a firefighter too! Your love, passion and dedication for the Fire Service fills me with immense pride everyday. I love and respect you beyond words.

And to you, the reader: if you made it this far, thank you. I hope you enjoyed reading my story as much as I enjoyed writing it. If you learned some safety tips along the way, awesome!

To everyone I've forgotten, thank you.

Last, but by no means least; to all the men and women of the Fire Service. You are my heroes. Thank you for all you do and the sacrifices you make every day. My dear friend Ricky once said; 'firefighters leave incidents, but incidents don't leave firefighters.' Never harbour your feelings, because it's OK not to be OK. And never be afraid to laugh, for laughter is the best medicine.

Credits

Trapeze would like to thank everyone at Orion who worked on the publication of *Up in Smoke*.

Agent
Rory Scarfe

Editor
Jamie Coleman

Copy-editor
Jane Donovan

Proofreader
Simon Fox

Editorial Management
Sarah Fortune
Jane Hughes
Charlie Panayiotou
Tamara Morriss
Claire Boyle

Audio
Paul Stark
Jake Alderson
Georgina Cutler

Contracts
Anne Goddard
Ellie Bowker

Design
Nick Shah
Tomas Almeida
Joanna Ridley
Helen Ewing

Finance
Nick Gibson
Jasdip Nandra

Sue Baker
Tom Costello

Inventory
Jo Jacobs
Dan Stevens

Marketing
Yadira Da Trindade

Production
Arianna Manzin
Katie Horrocks

Publicity
Elizabeth Allen

Sales
Jen Wilson
Victoria Laws
Esther Waters
Group Sales teams across
    Digital, Field Sales,
    International and
    Non-Trade

Operations
Group Sales Operations
    team

Rights
Susan Howe
Krystyna Kujawinska
Jessica Purdue
Ayesha Kinley
Louise Henderson